Also by John Gadway

Here Be Angels: Sojourn in a Different World
Mining and Migration in Guanacaste
My Huancayo Diary

Selected Consulting Reports

The Cameroon Credit Union Development Project
International Best Practices in Micro-Finance
The Demand for Deposit Facilities in Rural Ghana

Gadway received his PhD in German Literature from Tulane University in 1972 and his MA in Economics from Southern Illinois University in 1974. In the 1980s, based on work for the World Bank and other international donor agencies, he became known within certain circles in the development community for his discovery of the *Fundamental Theorem of Micro-Finance*—the statement of a natural law that defines limits to what can and what cannot be achieved by targeting the poorest of the poor in low-income countries with financial services. He retired from active consulting work at the end of 1990, when he married a local counterpart consultant from Indonesia. He is the father of four sons—ages 17, 19, 20 and 43 as of October 2013.

Work in Progress

The Axis of Evil: The Coming Anti-Copernican Revolution
Maxwell's Demon and Archimedes' Ghost
The Perfect Anthropic Principle
The Partition

The German Novel: A Theory
(2013)

Formerly

The Castle in the *Bildungsroman*

KaneBeGone, Inc., Miami

The Count, 1989

John Erik

Cover:

A Sketch of Germany
Karen Moty, San Gregorio, California

Photo of author on back cover:
By *Joanie*
Leesburg, Florida, July 2012

ISBN-13: 978-0-9895710-2-9
ISBN-10: 0-9895710-2-5
LCCN: 2014901173

Published by
KaneBeGone, Inc.
Miami, Florida

First *revised* edition, October 21, 2013

Original*: University Microfilms*, August 1972

10 9 8 7 6 5 4 3 2 1

For

Ingrid and John E.,

Who suffered with me,

And for Julie,[1]

Who clearly saw what I couldn't see.

---

[1] Not necessarily her real name.

CONTENTS

NOTES TO TODAY'S READER

To the student or general reader non-conversant in German

Perhaps 15% of the text of the dissertation is in German. As the thrust of the analysis does not depend crucially on these quotes, which serve essentially to substantiate what has been said in the English text, no effort has been made to translate these portions. On the other hand, translations are given for most of the German quotes presented in the Afterword, which is Chapter 4 of a work I recently published on a different subject. In that work (*Here Be Angels: Sojourn in a Different World*) there could be no presupposition that the readers would be acquainted with the original language.

To the expert

The Afterword just referred to was lifted verbatim from the book mentioned above. In *Here Be Angels* I discuss *Wilhelm Meister* from the perspective of Goethe the scientist. In this book I stress the fact, unknown to me at the time I was writing my dissertation, that Goethe valued his scientific work, particularly his *Farbenlehre*, more than all his literary output.

Digital Copy of the Original Dissertation is Available at:
http://www.louisianadigitallibrary.org/cdm/ref/collection/p16313
coll12/id/1194

PREFACE TO THE 40TH ANNIVERSARY EDITION

> *The prosperous middle classes, who ruled the
> nineteenth century, placed an excessive value upon
> placidity of existence. They refused to face the
> necessities for social reform imposed by the new
> industrial system, and they are now refusing to face the
> necessities for intellectual reform imposed by the new
> knowledge.*
>
> **Alfred North Whitehead**

Writing, I always thought, was my best skill, my long suit. Therefore, when Thomas Starnes, a member of my dissertation committee at Tulane, commented wryly that my writing would improve if I could banish the word "problem" from my vocabulary, I was stung. I shudder now, having just returned to that work of some 40 years ago, to imagine what an early draft of my dissertation must have looked like: that problematic word still turns up some sixty times in the final version he signed off on in the summer of 1972. Its staying power, however, may be justified by the subject matter addressed by the peculiarly German novel form that is the *Bildungsroman*. In my dissertation I argued that the great German novels of the first half of the twentieth century—Kafka's *Das Schloß*, Mann's *Zauberberg*, and Hesse's *Glasperlenspiel*—cannot be understood without appreciating the relatively unknown tradition in which they are rooted. Wieland's *Agathon*, Goethe's *Wilhelm Meister* in the late eighteenth century, and Stifter's *Nachsommer* in the mid-nineteenth, are the literary responses of their respective authors to the intensely felt problem confronting moral individuals facing

4

what Whitehead referred to as "the necessities for social reform imposed by the new industrial system."

The problem the writers of these *Bildungsromane* saw was the danger that the personal integrity of the morally driven social reformers was in danger of being undermined by the forces they sought to oppose or direct. The fact that these novels attempted to solve this problem by describing the appropriate formation (*Bildung*) of their heroes gives them a rather leaden, didactic feel, particularly to modern sensibilities; but they also provide a frame of reference and a vocabulary for the twentieth-century novelists who drew on and exploded this tradition.

On March 14, 1971, when I was writing my dissertation in absentia,[1] my *Doktorvater*, Margaret Groben, included a cover letter to me with her comments on Chapter 2. I remember reading the following excerpt from that letter with a sense of relief muted by a confusing feeling of dismay:

> As I never before have had a first draft that did not seem to me to need considerable overhauling, I have, underneath my pleasure in your work, the uneasy feeling that it can't be true, that I cannot have read it carefully enough! . . . Your study gives me a new view of the *Bildungsroman* and invalidates my idea of why . . . [it] . . . is no longer possible in its pristine form.

I felt relief because I, too, had had the uneasy feeling Groben described. I had noticed something that is so obvious—obvious, that is, once you notice it—that I felt I must have been dozing in class when they talked about this defining feature of the *Bildungsroman*. The confusing feeling of dismay is less easy to explain, but it was quite real.

---

[1] While on the faculty of the Department of Foreign Languages at Southern Illinois University—Carbondale.

Although I had, in effect, produced a theory of the *Bildungs-roman*, I wanted more. Dr. Groben's comment allowed overreaching ambitions smoldering beneath the surface to find a new supply of oxygen. After getting her letter I no longer wanted to write about this peculiarly German form of the novel. Rather, I wanted to take the problem that the eighteenth- and nineteenth-century German novelists had treated narrowly in specific historical contexts and analyze it in more general scientific terms. The day after I got the letter from the dean of the Graduate School confirming that I had been awarded my degree, I submitted my resignation to the Department of Foreign Languages at SIU-C and enrolled as a graduate student in the Department of Economics.

Economics, the "physics" of the social sciences, was, I imagined, the empirical bedrock on which the others were built. This is where I would find the mathematical tools and analytical concepts that would allow me "to face the necessities for intellectual reform imposed by the new knowledge" (Whitehead). Had I paid more attention to the dilemma identified by the writers of *Bildungsromane*, I could have saved myself a lifetime of wrong turns, defeats and frustration.

What I noticed about the six representative German novels I had chosen for closer analysis is that the principal character in each is an orphan or semi-orphan figure who, toward the end of what has been a rather disillusioning picaresque experience of his society, encounters a mentor or a foster-father figure in a castle or castle-like environment. In my analysis, what set the hero of these German novels apart from the picaroon of the earlier novel form to which the *Bildungsroman* is related was his genetic relationship to the "insider" figure of the even older tradition of the courtly novel. The traditional *Bildungsroman* hero, introduced by Wieland in *Agathon* and given definitive expression by Goethe in *Wilhelm Meister*, is the insider figure of the courtly tradition, who, while embracing the traditional moral values of his society, is forced by experience to view it from the outsider perspective of the picaroon, where its failings become manifest. Unlike the rogue of the picaresque tradition, however, the *Bildungsroman* hero—an optimistic and invariably somewhat naïve child of the Enlighten-ment—is not permitted to turn the unwritten rules by which the game is played to his own advantage. The picaroon, who typically meets his foster-father figure early in the novel, learns to survive—to preserve his physical person—by disregarding official social precepts and norms. To survive he must be a rogue.

The *Bildungsroman* hero inherits from the picaroon the challenge of personal survival, but in his case, for the insider, the trial is more subtle. He cannot, as it were, go over to the other side and use the unwritten rules of the game against his own community and nation. As a moral hero in the tradition of the courtly novel, he must affirm in his own person the highest values to which his society might aspire. More importantly, as a child of the Enlightenment, he must serve his society as a beacon of progress; he must lead by example. In other words, for the *Bildungsroman* hero, the problem of survival, particularly as it is reformulated by Goethe, is more complicated than it was for the picaroon. The rogue is challenged at the most basic level to keep body and soul together. The challenge facing the *Bildungsroman* hero is more existential: how to survive, not only physically, but with his personal integrity intact.

As Wieland formulated it in *Agathon* the problem was straight-forward—how to survive active engagement with society physically with one's personal integrity intact. As the problem was redefined by Goethe, it was not simply a matter of securing one's personal integrity against the dangers arising from a proactive engagement with society: Agathon seems to have received his fully-actualized moral self pretty much as a birthright. For the eponymous hero of

Goethe's great *Bildungsroman*, the problem was not merely one of preserving a personality against the dangers inherent in an active confrontation with society, but more fundamentally, of first achieving self-actualization in a society in which, according to Goethe, such *Bildung* was no longer a value.

Agathon, an active social reformer in the optimistic, pre-French-Revolution spirit of the Enlightenment, had to learn how to protect his personal integrity from the threats posed to it by the society he was attempting to reform. He had to learn the proper amount of contact with and isolation from the society in which he was embedded. The proper balance is instantiated both physically and symbolically by the castle of the important mentor he meets near the end of the novel. From within the confines of Archytas' thoughtfully appointed, garden-encircled villa, he can project the force of his personality onto the community as a whole without fear that it will be overwhelmed by the much greater force that is the common will. But when Wilhelm meets his various mentors and foster-father figures in their different castles in the final chapters of the *Lehrjahre*,[2] it is clear that the function of these castles is not merely to protect Wilhelm's personality from the dissipating forces unleashed by the French Revolution, but—especially in the instances that have the most bearing on Wilhelm's particular situation—to be a kind of cultural vault in which the treasures of European civilization are available to contribute to the formation of his personality, to his *Bildung*.

This extraliterary element in the German tradition gives the classic *Bildungsroman* a rather serious, moralizing tone, preventing novels in this tradition—particularly as it evolved in the nineteenth century—from becoming known or appreciated outside a rather

---

[2] Wilhelm had met some of them earlier in the novel, but the role as foster-father figure and mentor was not in evidence until he encountered them in their castles.

narrow slice of the German-speaking world. Then suddenly, in the first half of the twentieth century, with the work of Thomas Mann, Franz Kafka, Herman Hesse and others, the German novel takes its rightful place in the center of European literature.

It is not obvious that these great twentieth-century novels are *Bildungsromane*. Thomas Mann even referred to his *Zauberberg* as an anti-*Bildungsroman*. What Dr. Groben took from my dissertation is that it is not possible to evaluate these monumental works of Mann, Kafka and Hesse without seeing them in the context of the relatively unknown and peculiarly German novel form, the *Bildungsroman*.

When I started this project (in the fall of 1969) and gave the dissertation its original title—"The Castle in the Bildungsroman"— I thought I was headed for a discussion of Kafka's *Das Schloß* (*The Castle*). Kafka, at the time, was my favorite author writing in German, not because of the world he depicted that made the adjectival form of his name an internationally understood concept, but because of the crystalline purity of his prose. But a dissertation takes on a life of its own, which it nourishes by draining off some of the life of its author. By the end of the process, pretty much every PhD candidate in the humanities hates his or her topic and wants to be shut of it. Nobody on the committee was asking for more when I got through Thomas Mann and Hesse, so I let Kafka's *Castle* go. Perhaps some young Germanist will pick up the analysis where I left off and revisit Kafka's great novel fragment to determine where it may be found on the trajectory that rises from Wieland's *Agathon* through Goethe's *Wilhelm Meister*, falls in the nineteenth to Stifter's today practically unreadable *Nachsommer,* only to rise again in the twentieth century to true world-class status.

But now, on to my writing of some forty years ago. You will see overreaching efforts on the part of a graduate student to formulate general statements about impossibly complex trends in

European literary history. But you will also become aware of a general thrust and direction to the analysis that may give you a useful perspective for viewing the German tradition. I present a theory of the German novel which, like all good theories, is a caricature of the subject it attempts to capture in broad strokes. Theories are made to be modified and sometimes completely overthrown. That's what they are for. They are navigational aids. I hope this one may be of service to someone interested in understanding the peculiarly German novel form, the *Bildungsroman*.

John Gadway
Miami
October 21, 2013

Acknowledgments

Beyond the members of my dissertation committee at Tulane, all of whom I know for a fact to be deceased, particular thanks is due to Ingrid Gadway Clarke, for her careful reading of the manuscript, particularly the German portions, where she found hundreds of missing umlauts, diacritical marks, typos and other errors in my transcription of the type-written original. Special thanks is also due to my former colleague in crime and continuing friend, Dr. Lee Hartman, for his meticulous copy editing, for his patience with my inability to internalize the basics (much less the finer points) of any handbook of style, and for his frequent questioning of specific word choice, which was invariably on target.

Finally, I would like to thank Karen Moty for her help with cover design and preparation, not only for this book, but for her help with an earlier one, where her contribution went unacknowledged.

So that there is clarity on this subject, I repeat:

Thank you, Ingrid.

Thank you, Lee.

Thank you, Karen.

And thanks, again, Cousin Richard, for your help with the earlier book. And *gute Besserung*!

John Gadway
Miami
January 23, 2014

CHAPTER 1: A GERMAN TRADITION

L ike many other terms in the jargon of the literary historian, the term *Bildungsroman*, while enjoying wide use, is extremely imprecise. The problematical nature of the term is suggested by an examination of its component parts. The first element, *Bildung*, refers to a process that is highly structured or goal-oriented. The second element, *roman*, refers to a literary genre that is protean.[1] The two terms which combine to form *Bildungsroman* have themselves in time undergone tremendous semantic changes. *Bildung*, which in the age of Goethe designated an ideal of unquestioned validity, becomes in the nineteenth and twentieth centuries a concept of increasingly doubtful content. *Roman*, on the other hand, which was still for Schiller a term of disparagement, refers in the nineteenth and twentieth centuries to the highly respected, most popular and intensely cultivated of all the literary genres.[2]

The problem of defining the term *Bildungsroman* is compounded by the existence of several other related terms, which are themselves at best loosely defined. Some writers use the term *Entwicklungsroman* and *Erziehungsroman* as synonyms for *Bildungsroman*, whereas others use these two terms to limit and define it. Of those writers who use these three terms to designate closely related but distinct novel forms, most prefer to define

---

[1] Walter Pabst, "Literatur zur Theorie des Romans," *Deutsche Vierteljahrsschrift*, 34 (1960), 264.

[2] Friedrich Sengle—"Der Romanbegriff in der ersten Hälfte des 19. Jahrhunderts," in *Arbeiten zur deutschen Literatur 1750-1850* (Stuttgart: J. B. Metzlersche Verlagsbuchhandlung, 1965), p. 215—reminds us that the controversy over the artistic validity of literary works in prose actually continues well into the nineteenth century.

Bildungsroman and *Erziehungsroman* as sub-classes of the more general *Entwicklungsroman*.[3] Other writers, however, such as Werner Hoffmann,[4] turn the equation around and use the term *Bildungsroman* as the generic classification, making the *Entwicklungsroman* a modern sub-class of this genre. Still other writers, in their efforts to differentiate between the various novel forms, prefer to concentrate on just two of the terms to the neglect of the third. Lothar Köhn, for example, explicitly declines to include a discussion of the *Erziehungsroman* in his *Forschungsbericht*, "Entwicklungs- und Bildungsroman."[5] Heinrich Meyer, on the other hand, in the preface to the published dissertation by Helmut Germer, [6] confines himself to the problem of distinguishing between the *Erziehungsroman* and the *Bildungsroman*, to the complete neglect of the *Entwicklungsroman*. Finally, there is a group of writers who, like Herbert Ohl, use the term *Bildungsroman* in the sense of a *"Vermittlung von 'Entwicklungs-' und*

---

[3] Representatives of this group are: Melitta Gerhard, *Der deutsche Entwicklungsroman bis zu Goethes Wilhelm Meister* (Halle/Saale: Max Niemeyer Verlag, 1926; Gero von Wilpert, *Sachwörterbuch der Literatur*, 4th ed. (Stuttgart: Alfred Kröner Verlag, 1964)—entries *Bildungsroman*, *Entwicklungsroman*, and *Erziehungsroman*; Robert Petsch, „Wesen und Formen der Erzählkunst," *Deutsche Vierteljahrsschrift* Buchreihe, No. 20 (Halle/Saale: Max Niemeyer Verlag, 1934.

[4] „Grimmelshausens 'Simplizissimus' - nicht doch ein Bildungsroman?" *Germanisch-Romanische Monatsschrift*, N.F. 17 (1967), 172.

[5] „Entwicklungs- und Bildungsroman: Ein Forschungsbericht," *Deutsche Vierteljahrsschrift*, 42 (1968), 434.

[6] "The German Novel of Education 1792-1805: A Complete Bibliography and Analysis," in *German Studies in America*, 3, ed. Heinrich Meyer (Bern: Herbert Lang & Co., 1968.)

'Erziehungsroman.'"[7] The subjective moment of the *Entwicklungs-roman* is combined with the objective moment of the *Erziehungsroman*, both being then present in the *Bildungsroman*.

A formulation such as the one espoused by Ohl seems destined to bring order and clarity to the confusion of terms, for it makes a direct appeal to our common sense and our feeling for the meaning and impact of the words *Entwicklung*, *Erziehung*, and *Bildung*. Unfortunately such an *a priori* formulation does little more. For despite its precision of definition it is not possible to detect three distinct traditions or three separate groups of German novels that would correspond to the divisions: *Bildungsroman*, *Entwicklungsroman*, and *Erziehungsroman*. [8] Nevertheless, generations of researchers have, like Ohl, allowed a consideration of the various and changing meanings of words such as *Bildung*, *Entwicklung*, and *Erziehung* to cloud their investigation of the *Bildungsroman*. [9] If the term *Bildungsroman* is to be retained as

---

[7] Herbert Ohl, *Bild und Wirklichkeit: Studien zur Romankunst Raabes und Fontanes* (Heidelberg: Lothar Stiehm Verlag, 1968), p. 259.

[8] In view of the persistent elusiveness of a generally acceptable definition of the term *Bildungsroman* some scholars are inclined to dispense with it altogether. Köhn, p. 463, for example, cites the attitude of skepticism that Günther Weydt, Rudolf Mayut, and Fritz Martini maintain towards the category *Bildungsroman*.

[9] Berta Berger, for example, („Der moderne deutsche Bildungsroman, Sprache und Dichtung": *Forschungen zur Sprach- und Literaturwis-senschaft*, No. 69, ed. Harry Mayne, Fritz Strich, and S. Singer [Berne-Leipzig: Paul Haupt, Akademische Buchhandlung, 1942], p. 1), begins her study of the modern *Bildungsroman* with a discussion of the meaning and etymology of the word *Bildung*. Hans Heinrich Borcherdt provides in his article on the *Bildungsroman* (*Reallexikon der deutschen Literatur-geschichte,* founded by Paul Merker and Wolfgang Stammler, 2nd ed. [Berlin: Walter de Gruyter & Co., 1958]. I, 176) at one and the same time a brief history as well as an example of the confusion which arises from a too close consideration of the popular meanings of the terms: "Hierfür

having usefulness and validity for the literary historian, it must refer, without regard to non-literary-historical meanings or implications of the word *Bildung*, to some definable novel form or traditions for which no preferable term has been found. A definition of the *terminus technicus Bildungsroman* should therefore begin with an examination of the representative *Bildungsromane*.

At this point the researcher is confronted with the dilemma which lies at the heart of Karl Viëtor's much-cited article,

---

erweist sich der Begriff der 'Bildung' als Ausdruck der Selbstformung der Persönlichkeit als zu eng gefasst . . . Daher wurde in einer Reihe von Arbeiten der allgemeinere Begriff 'Entwicklungsroman' eingeführt . . . Noch weniger aber vermag der Begriff ‚Erziehungsroman' das Wesen dieser Dichtungsform zu umschreiben. Denn ‚Erziehung' ist in der Pädagogik die von außen kommende Beeinflussung des Werdeganges eines jungen Menschen, während die Bildungsromane das menschliche Werden unter dem Gesichtspunkt spontaner Eigenkraft, Selbsttätigkeit und Eigengesetzlichkeit darstellen, also unter den Prinzipien, die die Pädagogik als Wachstum bezeichnet. Da nun aber die moderne Erziehungswissenshaft sich bemüht, den im 19. Jahrhundert zum bloßen Wissen entwerteten Bildungsbegriff wieder zur Höhe der Pestalozzischen Auffassung emporzusteigen, die darunter die Formung der Seele durch die Mittel der umgebenden Kultur versteht, so besteht kein Anlaß, von dem eingebürgerten Begriff abzugehen." In a recent monograph, François Jost („La Tradition du ‚Bildungsroman,' *Comparative Literature*, 21 [1969], 98-99) betrays a similar concern for the meaning of the term *Bildung* : « Il faut s'arrêter d'abord au terme. On pourrait, on devrait même rappeler le sens premier de Bildung, synonyme, jusqu'au dix-huitième siècle, de Bild, d'imago, de portrait. Bildung (formation), au sens pédagogique, pour ainsi dire, du terme, est le processus par lequel l'être humain devient l'image de l'agent, s'identifie avec son modèle, avec son créateur. »

"Probleme der literarischen Gattungsgeschichte."[10] For if on the one hand it seems inadvisable to proceed to a definition of a genre such as *Bildungsroman* without first examining the representatives of that genre, it seems impossible on the other to determine the representatives of a tradition or genre without resort to the criteria that a definition would provide. As a solution to this impasse Viëtor suggests the method first proposed by Schleiermacher, whereby one begins with a provisionary, intuitive hypothesis of the entirety, the genre, before turning to a close examination of the individuals, the novels, which in turn provide the basis for a refinement or modification of the original hypothesis.[11] The Alexandrian stroke which provides the solution to this dilemma, however, the original, intuitive hypothesis, is at once the strength and the weakness of the method, for to a large extent the value of the objective facts that such a synthetic-analytic method may provide is predetermined by the "rightness" of the researcher's intuition.

The first intuitive hypothesis that we will make regarding the category or genre *Bildungsroman* is that the term refers to a *peculiarly German novel form*, which first appears in the latter half of the eighteenth century and which continues to be cultivated in

---

[10] Karl Viëtor, "Probleme der literarischen Gattungsgeschichte," *Deutsche Vierteljahrsschrift*, 9 (1931), 425-447.
[11] Viëtor, "Probleme," p. 442.

various modes well into the twentieth century.[12] Wilhelm Dilthey,[13] who first made the term the center of a wide literary discussion, did not explicitly restrict its application to German works. Nevertheless, he used this term to designate the German novel of the age of Goethe and he was conscious of the German origin of the form.[14] He expressly calls attention to the distinctions that exist between *Bildungsromane* and earlier, only superficially related novel forms such as biographical novels, [15] of which he cites Fielding's *Tom Jones* as a prime example. Other writers contributed further to the view that the term *Bildungsroman* refers to a

---

[12] Using the terminology of Eberhard Lammert—*Bauformen des Erzählens* (Stuttgart: J. B. Metzlersche Verlagsbuchhandlung, 1955), p. 16—*Bildungsroman* in our definition would thus refer to an historical *genre* rather than a type: "In aller Mischung wandeln sich diese Typen selbst nicht, wie es die Gattungen und selbst die ‚Gattungshaftigkeiten' mit der Zeit tun ... Gattungen sind für uns historische Leitbegriffe, Typen sind ahistorische Konstanten." Such a conception of the *Bildungsroman* is basically in agreement with the suggestion made by Lothar Köhn, p. 435: "Auf diese Weise würden sich die beiden Begriffe zwei Kategorien-Systemen zuordnen: ‚Bildungsroman' benennt eine konkrete historische Gattung oder Dichtungsart, ‚Entwicklungsroman' dagegen einen quasi-überhistorischen Aufbautypus, womit zwei Blickrichtungen angegeben sind, die, obwohl sie seit einiger Zeit geläufig, bisher für die Klärung der umstrittenen Begriffe nicht ausdrücklich genutzt wurden."
[13] Although, as Fritz Martini has demonstrated—"Der Bildungsroman: Zur Geschichte der Theorie und des Wortes," *Deutsche Vierteljahrsschrift*, 35 (1961), 44-63—Morgenstern was the first to use the term, he did not secure for it a place in the mainstream of literary-historical discussion. He used the term to refer to the modern novel form per se, and gradually broadened it to include representatives from all literatures.
[14] Wilhelm Dilthey, *Das Erlebnis und die Dichtung: Lessing, Goethe, Novalis, Hölderlin*, 7th ed. (Leipzig und Berlin: Verlag B. G. Teubner, 1921), p. 393
[15] Dilthey, pp. 394-95.

specifically German novel form, [16] until finally the *Bildungsroman* came to be considered "die deutsche Großform des Romans überhaupt."[17]

The existence of a large number of foreign novels which are frequently termed *Bildungsromane* by various scholars does not constitute a serious challenge to the "rightness" of our first intuitive hypothesis. These scholars proceed as a rule from an *a priori* definition of the term *Bildungsroman* based largely on a consideration of the meaning of the term *Bildung* (or *Entwicklung*, or *Erziehung*) and, as a group, use the term loosely.[18]

After the formulation of our first intuitive hypothesis the next step is to examine the individual novels. Since we framed our original hypothesis very broadly, however, it is impossible to examine all individual works theoretically deserving consideration. A selection must be made, despite the erosion of objectivity which

---

[16] Karl Viëtor, for example—*Goethe* (Bern: A. Francke AG Verlag, 1949), p. 133—calls the *Bildungsroman* "die deutsche Spezies des modernen Romans."

[17] Hans Heinrich Borcherdt, *Reallexikon der deutschen Literaturgeschichte*, I, 175. Walter Müller-Seidel summarizes this point of view as follows: „Was sich als Leistung eindrucksvoll darbietet, bleibt mittelbar oder unmittelbar der Romanform des Goethe'schen ‚Wilhelm Meister' verpflichtet . . . Die Geschichte des deutschen Romans ist weithin identisch mit derjenigen des deutschen Bildungsromans." („Fontane: ‚Der Stechlin,'" in *Der deutsche Roman,* ed. Benno von Wiese [Düsseldorf: August Bagel Verlag, 1963], II, 147-48) Most recently, François Jost—„La Tradition du ‚Bildungsroman,'" 106—has restated this viewpoint, which may be regarded as a truism concerning the *Bildungsroman*: „En fait, tout roman allemand qui présente une certaine *Weltanschauung* appartient, à partir de *Meister*, de près ou de loin, au genre que nous étudions."

[18] See, for example, the broad definition adopted by Hans R. Wagner, *Der englische Bildungsroman bis in die Zeit des ersten Weltkrieges* (Bern: A. Francke Verlag, 1951, p. 13, ff.

such a choosing necessarily involves. Again we must rely to a certain extent on our intuition, but now it is imperative that we allow an *opinio communis* to guide and correct our intuition.[19]

As part of an effort to limit and define the subject of his own investigation of the *Trivialroman*, Martin Greiner remarks that the representative German novels of modern times are *Bildungs-romane*, and refers to the peculiarly German nature of these novels. His suggestion of the oneness of the concept, "the specifically German form of the modern novel" and the *Bildungsroman*, is so closely related to our original hypothesis concerning the *Bildungsroman* (that it is a peculiarly German novel form) that his comments deserve to be quoted in full:

> Gerade dieses Darüberhinauswachsen begründet die spezifische Entwicklung unserer Literatur ins Hochgesteigert-Individuelle, so daß man sagen kann, die spezifisch deutsche Form des modernen Romans sei der Entwicklungs- oder Bildungsroman. Die repräsentativen deutschen Romane der neueren Zeit, angefangen von Wielands *Agathon* über *Wilhelm Meister*, den *Nachsommer, den Grünen Heinrich*, bis zu Thomas Manns *Zauberberg* und Hesses *Glasperlenspiel*, sind Bildungsromane. Ihre Fundamente so tief gegraben und ihre Stockwerke so hoch getürmt, daß der Boden, von dem sie sich abheben, kaum noch ins Auge fählt; die großen deutschen Romane wachsen in die Höhe oder Tiefe, nicht in die Breite; sie sind leicht und hoch oder auch tief und finster, aber ohne Weltweite und Geräumigkeit. Sie sind nicht das, was der

---

[19]Lothar Köhn, *Entwicklungs- und Bildungsroman*, p. 445, has suggested that the decision whether any given novel be considered a *Bildungsroman* be surrendered to a gradually evolving *opinio communis*.

moderne Roman auch sein muß: sie sind nicht eigentlich populär.[20]

The six novels mentioned here by Greiner will form the basis for our further investigation of this phenomenon *Bildungsroman*. For although the appropriateness of the designation *Bildungsroman* has been disputed for a number of these novels by several reputable Germanists,[21] there exists a very substantial *opiniono communis* which states, first, that these six novels are "representative German novels," and that these novels are indeed *Bildungsromane*.[22]

****

---

[20] Martin Greiner, *Die Entstehung der modernen Unterhaltungsliteratur: Studien zum Trivialroman des 18. Jahrhunderts* (Reinbek bei Hamburg: Rowohlt Taschenbuch Verlag GmbH, 1964, pp. 32-33.)

[21] Lothar Köhn, p. 441, writes: „Kayser und Schlechta haben den ‚Lehrjahren,' Staiger hat dem ‚Nachsommer' dem Charakter eines Bildungsromans abgesprochen—mit dem Argument, dem Helden fehle die ‚Individualität.'"

[22] For example, Werner Hoffmann, "Grimmelshausens ‚Simplizissimus,'" p. 178, refers to all but *Zauberberg* as *Bildungsromane*. Gero von Wilpert, *Sachwörterbuch*, p. 166, also cites as examples all but *Zauberberg*. Roy Pascal—*The German Novel* (Toronto: University of Toronto Press, 1956), p. 166—devotes the first part of his book to a discussion of the *Bildungsromane* of Goethe, Keller, Stifter and Thomas Mann. The article "Bildungsroman" in *Der Große Brockhaus*—16th ed. (1953), II, 122—cites *Agathon, Wilhelm Meister, Nachsommer* and *Der Grüne Heinrich* as examples of *Bildungsromane*. Herbert Seidler in „Wandlung des deutschen Bildungsromans im 19. Jahrhundert," *Wirkendes Wort*, 11 (1961), 148-62, cites all but *Agathon*.

When one considers the six novels mentioned above as the representatives of a group or a tradition, several generic characteristics become apparent at once. Perhaps the first generally valid observation that can be made concerning the nature of the *Bildungsroman* is that each novel presents the story of the growth, development, or education of the central figure from some point of relative ignorance and immaturity to some point of awareness and maturity. Closer attention to the biography of the central figures reveals a further striking characteristic common to all these six novels: This central figure is a quasi-orphan figure. In four of the six novels—*Agathon*, *Der Grüne Heinrich*, *Zauberberg*, and *Glasperlenspiel*—the orphanhood of the main character, either real or supposed, is apparent. In *Wilhelm Meister* it is suggested first by the tension which exists between Wilhelm and his father and further by the death of Wilhelm's grandfather, whose spiritual and intellectual heir Wilhelm is,[23] before the report of the actual death of his father occurs in Book 5. Stifter's *Nachsommer* constitutes the only seeming exception to this rule, for Heinrich Drendorf stands in a very clear, ideally filial relationship to his real father. *Nachsommer* is, however, the exception which proves the rule, for we note that the "plot" of this novel, in the barest outline, is the story of Heinrich's gradual removal from his parental home to the home of his "foster father," Risach.

---

[23]Thomas P. Saine, "Wilhelm Meister's Homecoming," *Journal of English and Germanic Philosophy*, 69, No. 3 (1970), 464: "The Abbé imagines that if the grandfather's art collection had not been sold after his death Wilhelm's reaction might have been different. . . Since, however, . . . the collection was sold, it could not be an instrument of his education, but has become instead a symbol of his loss (but something which is to be regained in the end of the novel)." The fact that Wilhelm does not possess this heritage from his grandfather seems to underline his status as an orphan figure.

In the figure of Risach, whom many writers consider to be the main character in the novel, we recognize another of the characteristics of the *Bildungsroman*. In each of these six novels there is at least one foster-father figure, who exerts or seeks to exert direct influence on the development of the hero and who frequently represents (often alternative) ideals toward which the hero develops or strives, or between which he is to choose. The importance of such figures in the six novels in our survey, from Hippias and Archytas in *Agathon*, Jarno and Abbé in *Wilhelm Meister*, including Römer and the *Graf* in *Der Grüne Heinrich*, Risach in *Nachsommer*, Settembrini, Behrens, and Naphta in *Zauberberg*, and finally a whole host of such figures in *Glasperlenspiel* strongly suggests that the presence of at least one foster-father figure is a sine qua non for the *Bildungsroman*. A heuristic definition of the *Bildungsroman* must seek to explain the thematic and formal role of this fundamental element of all *Bildungsromane*.

Still another similarity in the six novels is a basic underlying similarity in structure, which, although not immediately apparent, may well be the single most important characteristic of the *Bildungsroman*. The hero, in his progress from a state of relative ignorance and youthful naïveté to one of relative wisdom and maturity, experiences the world in two distinct fashions. He experiences the world as "experienced" world and as "presented" world. In the first mode of world-experience or world-encounter the hero knows only what his experience and his wits tell him. The world appears unstructured, fluid, baffling, in a word, "real." In the second mode of world-encounter the hero is not present as experiencer but rather as observant, potential disciple. The world is a structured world, an ideal or concept of the world. It is presented, unraveled, and explained before his eyes. In the first instance the world is experienced in time, and thus necessarily in part. In the second instance the world is viewed from without as an entirety or at least from the perspective of some unifying principle. The importance of the foster-father figure in this latter mode of world-experience is, of course, paramount.

The distinction between the two modes of world-encounter and the importance that such a distinction can have for the structure of the *Bildungsroman* can be demonstrated with the example of *Agathon*. When we first meet our hero he has just suffered banishment from the city of Athens. In the mountains of Thrakia he almost falls victim to a group of frantic Bacchantes before they all in turn become the captives of a group of marauding pirates attracted by the noise of the reveling. On board the pirate ship he finds his long lost Psyche, disguised as a boy. Before they can plan their escape, however, Agathon is transshipped to Smyrna, where he is sold as a slave to Hippias. Up until this point the world as it is represented in the novel has been presented in terms of Agathon's individual experiences. When Agathon enters the well-ordered house of Hippias, however, he no longer experiences the "world," but a vision of it, Hippias' particular Weltanschauung. He observes this world and adopts a critical stance with respect to it. When Hippias is absent for a while Agathon begins once again to "experience" the world, first in the form of a confusing, deeply emotional erotic relationship to Danae, then in his demoralizing experiences as a political and social reformer in Syracuse. When Agathon arrives in Tarent, he once again observes the world as an entirety in terms of Archytas' Weltanschauung. Agathon accepts without critical hesitation or reserve this vision of the world, which, while it "explains" his experience of the world, provides a counterbalance to the convincing but unacceptable philosophy of Hippias, thereby "reconciling" a disillusioned Agathon with society.

The novel ends with a sketch of Agathon's life in Tarent, for it is here that the orphan stops his wandering, here that he finds a home. In a sense it is a homecoming for Agathon. In Tarent he finds not only a foster father, "einen zweiten Vater,"[24] but his only living blood relative, his sister Psyche. *Agathon* thus exhibits a structure-thematic peculiarity discoverable in the six *Bildungsromane* in our survey. The "homecoming" in *Der Grüne Heinrich*, for example, is unmistakable,[25] and recently Professor Saine has called attention to a similar phenomenon in *Wilhelm Meister*.[26] All six novels end approximately where they begin, perhaps on a higher level, but, viewed from above, a circle has been described. Agathon, the sometime political leader of Athens, whom we met just after his banishment from his native *Vaterstadt,* Athens, devotes himself to the public affairs of his adopted *Vaterstadt*, the model Republic of Tarent. Wilhelm Meister, who in the beginning flees the bourgeois confinement of the parental home and his father's business, accepts willingly in the end the responsibilities and duties of parenthood and of membership in a community.[27] Heinrich Lee

---

[24] Christoph Martin Wieland, *Ausgewählte Werke in drei Bänden*, ed. Friedrich Beißner (Munich: Winkler Verlag, 1964), II, 458. Unless otherwise indicated, all subsequent references to Wieland's works will be to the Beißner edition.

[25] See Seidler, *Wandlungen des deutschen Bildungsromans*, p. 156: „Trotzdem wird die gesamte Raumstruktur schon 1854 deutlich: von der Heimat aus—in die Heimat zurück."

[26] Saine, "Wilhelm Meister's Homecoming," pp. 450-69.

[27] Goethe writes of Wilhelm in Book 8 (This and all subsequent references to *Wilhelm Meister* are to Johann Wolfgang von Goethe, *Werke*, ed. Erich Trunz, 5th ed. [Hamburg: Christian Wegner Verlag, 1962], p. 502: " . . . und mit dem Gefühl des Vaters hatte er auch alle Tugenden eines Bürgers erworben." Although the word „Bürger" may be understood in the class-distinguishing sense of „bourgeois," I think that Goethe is using it here in the sense of "citizen." "Bürgerliche Tugenden" then would be virtues desirable or necessary for membership in a community, such as respect for the rights of others, willingness to contribute to the common good, etc.

likewise returns home to discharge his duties as a public servant. Hans Castorp returns to the "flatlands" to serve his country in its dubious endeavors. Joseph Knecht leaves Kastalien to serve as a teacher the society he had earlier deserted as a pupil. Again *Nachsommer* seems to be the exception to the general rule. There is a "homecoming" in this novel, however; the circle is closed, not by the return of Heinrich to Vienna, but by the retirement of Heinrich's father from his business and his withdrawal to a country estate in the vicinity of the *Rosenhaus* and the *Sternenhof*.

The circular structure observable in all six of these novels provides the formal counterpart to what many writers consider the central thematic moment of the *Bildungsroman*, namely the reconciliation of the individual with society.[28] The individual who in the beginning is "banished" from his society or who voluntarily departs from it, returns in the end, "reconciled," to do it service.

The definition formulated by Roy Pascal, that the *Bildungsroman* is "the story of the formation of a character up to the moment when he ceases to be self-centered and becomes society-centered,"[29] seems to be warranted by our observations. It seems possible and even necessary, however, to modify this definition to a certain extent. The *Bildungsroman* is not merely the story of the formation of *a* character, but the story of a *particular kind of* character, an orphan figure. The hero of the *Bildungsroman* initially stands alone in the world. Also, as noted, the formation of this character takes place under the influence of two distinct modes of world-encounter, as firsthand experiences of the world as reality, and as idea, in terms of the *Weltanschauung* of one or more foster-father figures.

---

[28] Köhn, "Entwicklungs- und Bildungsroman," pp. 455-56.
[29] Pascal, *The German Novel*, p. 11.

The encounter of the orphan hero with the father figure or figures in the realm of the "presented" world we shall refer to as his "castle experience," to distinguish this type of world-encounter from his immediate experience of the world. For the realm in which the hero experiences the *Weltanschauung* of the father figure is typically a mansion, a castle, or a castle-like retreat.[30] In *Agathon*, for example, we find the sharply contrasting mansions of Hippias and Archytas; in *Wilhelm Meister,* the castles of Lothario and the *Oheim*, to mention just the most important castles; in *Der Grüne Heinrich,* the castle of the *Graf*; in *Nachsommer,* principally the *Rosenhaus*; in *Zauberberg,* on the one hand, the sanatorium itself, on the other, the modest lodgings of Settembrini and Naphta; and finally in *Glasperlenspiel*, Kastalien in its entirety, as well as the monastery. This "castle experience," which is obviously a central, pivotal experience for every *Bildungsroman* hero, will form the basis and focal point for our further investigation of these six novels and the phenomenon *Bildungsroman*.

Before proceeding with our investigation we should note that the castle as a literary device is related to the "poetic island" which Horst Brunner treats in his monograph, *Die poetische Insel*, and even more closely to the poetic space which Brunner discusses under the rubric "quasi-island," and sees as sharing the main characteristics of the poetic space of the island. [31] The chief

---

[30]Even when, as in *Wilhelm Meister*, the encounter of the orphan figure with the foster-father figure takes place in a tavern (the "stranger," p. 68ff.), or on the road (the Abbé, p. 119ff.), these father figures are emissaries of another world. Their significance becomes apparent to the hero and to the reader only when they are viewed in their relationship to this other realm.

[31]Horst Brunner, *Die poetische Insel: Inseln und Inselvorstellungen in der deutschen Literatur,* Germanistische Abhandlungen, No. 21 (Stuttgart: J. B. Metzlersche Verlagsbuchhandlung, 1967), p. 28

function of poetic islands in a literary work is, according to Brunner, to express graphically (*"bildhaft"*) the relationship of the individual to his society. Poetic islands are well suited to this function because the poetic space of an island may be interpreted subjectively either positively, as asylum, or negatively, as exile, depending on the individual's relationship to the outside world.[32] A positively interpreted island, which reflects an individual's dissatisfaction with his society, Brunner refers to as a "flucht-utopische" island, while he refers to a negatively interpreted one as a "Robinsonadeninsel."

According to Brunner this function of poetic islands accounts for their prevalence in world literature during periods of transition, such as the transition from the Middle Ages to the Renaissance, when the relationship of the individual to society has become problematical.[33] The comparative scarcity of the poetic islands in medieval literature, for example, and the generally negative interpretation of such islands when they do occur, reflects the relatively greater stability of medieval society and the more positive relationship of the medieval poet to this society. The baroque mistrust of society, on the other hand, is reflected in a series of positively interpreted "fluchtutopische" islands.[34]

Brunner distinguishes carefully between the "fluchtutopische" island and a third type of island, that of the social utopia.[35] Brunner argues that the island of the social utopia is not a true "poetic"

---

[32]Brunner, p. 74ff.

[33]Brunner, pp. 242-43.

[34]Brunner, p. 90.

[35] Since, as Brunner notes, p. 141, the "fluchtutopische" island is characteristic for German literature in the 18th century, to the virtual exclusion of the island of the social utopia—as well as the "Robinsonadeninsel"—the distinctions that he lists between the two types are of some interest to us as we begin to examine the novels of Wieland and Goethe.

island because it does not serve to illustrate the relationship of the hero to society, but is concerned only with society and its future change.[36] Common to both the "fluchtutopische" island and the island of the social utopia is the explicit or implicit criticism of society and the establishment of some idealized alternative society on the island. The "Fluchtutopie," however, carries the implication that any attempt to change the existing society is futile. Hence the emphasis on emigration. The social utopia, on the other hand, springs from the assumption or the hope that society is perfectible or at least improvable. The two types are further differentiated by the characteristic make-up of the society on the islands. Whereas the "Sozialutopie" describes an ideal state as a model for changing the existing social order, the "Fluchtutopie" typically describes an idyllic community of kindred souls who have fled the hopelessly oppressive conditions of contemporary society.

The discussion in the following chapters of the "castle experience" in the novels selected for closer examination should answer the questions: Do the castles in these novels have the same structural and thematic functions that Brunner has outlined for the poetic islands? Are these castles adequately described as "quasi-islands," or do they have related but different functions which are more suited to the needs and the ends of the *Bildungsroman*? The use of islands to illustrate the problematical relationship of the

---

[36]Brunner, p. 112: "Neben diesen beiden poetischen Inselformen, . . . gibt es noch die Sonderform der sozialutopischen Insel, die sich in staatsphilosophischen Traktaten findet, weder Exil not Asyl bedeutet und nicht im bestehenden geographischen Raum gedacht ist. Sie ist ein Gegenmodell zur bestehenden geschichtlichen Situation. In ihr geht es nicht wie bei den anderen beiden Inselformen um das Verhältnis von ‚Drinnen' (Insel; Ich) und ‚Draußen' (Welt; Gesellschaft), sondern allein um die künftige Veränderung der bestehenden Wirklichkeit, also allein um das ‚Draußen.'"

individual to society, for example, seems to lend itself naturally to exploitation in the *Bildungsroman*, which is, as we have seen, concerned with the reconciliation of the individual to society. On the other hand, many of the castles in these novels are exemplary in nature, and thus seem to be related to the "non-poetic" island of the social utopia. And what is the significance of the fact that all of the "castles" in our six novels, in contradistinction to the typical "poetic islands," are inhabited before the arrival of the main character and that these inhabitants exist in a definite relation to and in constant contact with society, with the outside world?

The answers to these and similar questions should provide the insights necessary for a further definition of the term *Bildungsroman*. Close attention to the changing role and nature of the castles in the novels during the eighteenth and nineteenth centuries should make it possible to sketch the evolution of this German novel form up to the dawn of the twentieth century in terms of its most persistent features, the "castle experience" of the hero—the pivotal encounter of the orphan figure with one or more foster-father figures. It should also be possible, by recognizing the evolution of this central feature of the classic Bildungsroman in the novels of Thomas Mann and Hermann Hesse, to make some general statements about the development of the tradition in the twentieth century.

Because we are concerned primarily with the origin and the evolution of a tradition, relatively more space will be allotted to the earlier representatives of the tradition, and to the relationship of the German tradition to older European novel traditions. Thus an entire chapter will be devoted to the relationship of the *Bildungsroman* tradition to the tradition of the picaresque novel. *Agathon* and *Wilhelm Meister* will be analyzed each in a separate chapter, but the representatives of this "middle" tradition, *Nachsommer* and *Der Grüne Heinrich*, will be discussed together in the fifth chapter. The concluding chapter will attempt to indicate how the great *Bildungsromane* of Mann and Hesse represent a coming to terms with the problems that lie at the heart of the German tradition, and to suggest the direction that a fuller investigation of this tradition in the twentieth century might take. Such an investigation would certainly include a close analysis not only of *Zauberberg* and *Glasperlenspiel*, but also of the great novel fragments of Kafka.

AN EINEN WELTVEBESSERER

"Alles opfert' ich hin," sprichst du, "der
Menschheit zu helfen;

Eitel war der Erfolg, Haß und Verfolgung
der Lohn."—

Soll ich dir sagen, Freund, wie ich mit
Menschen es halte?

Traue dem Spruche! Noch nie hat mich
der Führer getauscht:

Von der Menschheit—du kannst von ihr
nie groß genug denken;

Wie du im Busen sie trägst, prägst du in
Taten sie aus.

Auch dem Menschen, der dir im engen
Leben begegnet,

Reich ihm wenn er sie mag, freundlich die
helfende Hand.

Nur für Regen und Tau und fürs Wohl der
Menschengeschlechter

Laß du den Himmel, Freund, sorgen wie
gestern so heut.

Schiller

CHAPTER 2: A EUROPEAN TRADITION

The many similarities that exist between the early representatives of the German *Bildungsroman* and the picaresque novel are so apparent that most writers have felt compelled to call our attention to the more striking dissimilarities. Gero von Wilpert, for example, stresses the picaroon's relative lack of individuality compared with the hero of the *Bildungsroman*.[1] Wilfried van der Will, on the other hand, contrasts the speed with which the picaroon becomes acquainted with the wiles of society to the painfully slow development of the typical *Bildungsroman* hero.[2] The many similarities, however, are so persuasive, that we feel compelled to examine the nature of the relationship between these two literary traditions before proceeding with our own investigation of the *Bildungsroman* and the "castle experience" of its orphan hero.

The most obvious point of contact between these two novel forms is, of course, their underlying structure: Both novel forms present at least part of the life story of one central figure. In the *Bildungsroman*, as we have seen, this central figure is typically an orphan, who, despite occasional appearances to the contrary, is basically alone in the world. The picaroon, too, is typically an orphan and a basically lonely character.[3]

---

[1] Von Wilpert, *Sachwörterbuch*, p. 622.

[2] Wilfried van der Will, *Pikaro heute; Metamorphose des Schelms bei Thomas Mann, Döblin, Brecht, Grass* (Stuttgart: W. Kohlhammer Verlag, 1967), p. 14.

[3] A number of writers have stressed this point, including: Robert Alter, *Rogue's Progress: Studies in the Picaresque Novel*, Harvard Studies in Comparative Literature, No. 26 (Cambridge, Mass.: Harvard University Press, 1964). Alter cites the unpublished dissertation by Claudio

The solitude of the central character in picaresque novels is an expression of his position outside society.[4] To cite Robert Alter: "The picaresque novel . . . is born out of the conflict between the individual and his society.[5] The underlying theme of the *Bildungs-roman* was defined above as the resolution of the conflict between the individual and the world, the reconciliation of the hero to society. That is, it reflects a similar polarization of the individual versus the world.

As Horst Brunner noted, the question of the relationship of the individual to society gains special relevance during and after periods of great social change.[6] Roy Pascal, referring to four of the six novels in our survey, argues that "all the *'Bildungsromane'* were written in the aftermath of revolution and social turmoil,"[7] thereby suggesting a further point of contact between the picaresque novel and the *Bildungsroman*, for, as several scholars have noted, picaresque novels, too, appear characteristically in periods of transition. Oskar Seidlin writes that "Picaro was born when an empire . . . was gradually being undermined by slow . . . decay; when values and institutions whose strength was still proclaimed had step by step fallen victims to doubt and corruption . . . The

---

Guillén—"The Anatomies of Roguery," Harvard 1953, p. 383—"The basic situation of the picaresque novel is the solitude of its principal character in the world."

Oskar Seidlin, "Picaresque Elements in Thomas Mann's Work," *Essays in German and Comparative Literature*, 30 (Chapel Hill, N.C.: University of North Carolina Press, 1961), pp. 168-69: "Picaro . . . is always and basically an orphan, which in his case is not simply a matter of the premature disappearance of his parents, but the true and tragic signature of his existence."

[4] Alter, p. 71. "The picaroon, before all else, is an outsider."

[5] Alter, p. 107.

[6] Cf. note 33, Chapter 1.

[7] Pascal, *The German Novel*, p. 97

scenery upon which the Picaro moves is an empire on the eve of destruction."[8] And Robert Alter sees in the figure of the picaroon a new insistence on individuality, which he traces in part to the incipient breakdown of the medieval community.[9]

Despite the central position of the picaroon in the picaresque novel, the figure of the hero is not actually the subject of main interest. As Robert Alter writes:

> The picaresque novel is a form of narrative which is concerned with action and the external world . . . The events and motions of this struggle are the principal interest; not the personality of the struggler, which is never even highly particularized. We are allowed to see the world through the eyes of a moderately interesting and believable individual, but it is the world that we are supposed to see, not *his* world; he—his inner life, his psychological complexity, his moral growth or decline—is not allowed to come between us and the large world.[10]

Although the personality of the hero of the *Bildungsroman* is considerably more "highly particularized" than that of the picaroon, although we are interested in *his* world, the personality of the hero, like that of the picaroon, is not the central interest in the *Bildungsroman*. Thomas Mann reminds us at the very beginning of *Zauberberg* that he is telling the story of Hans Castorp "nicht um seinetwillen (denn der Leser wird einen einfachen, wenn auch ansprechenden jungen Menschen in ihm kennenlernen),

---

[8] Seidlin, p. 163. Note the similarity of the formulation by Robert Alter—*Rogue's Progress*, p. 66—"The typical background for the picaresque novel is a world where the old social order is disintegrating but is still regarded as though it were continuing undisturbed."
[9] Alter, p. 51.
[10] Alter, p. 31.

sondern um der Geschichte willen."[11] The fictitious biographer of Joseph Knecht tells us at the start that he is more interested in his subject as "Typen denn als Einzelperson."[12] The personality of Heinrich Drendorf does not thrust itself to the center of our attention, despite the first person form of narration. Victor Lange goes so far as to argue that "Heinrich ist nicht der Gegenstand, sondern das Mittel des Erzählens."[13] Both Wolfgang Kayser and Karl Schlechta have argued that the figure of Wilhelm Meister lacks individuality.[14] The ironic distance that Wieland maintains with respect to Agathon, much like the attitude of Thomas Mann towards Hans Castorp, is in itself indication enough that he is not concerned primarily with the personality of his main character.

In only one of the six novels in our survey is the main interest born principally by a concern for the personality of the central figure. Just why Keller's *Der Grüne Heinrich* should prove the exception to this general rule is an interesting question which, in view of Keller's non-German citizenship, may well provide a hint for further refinement of our definition of the *Bildungsroman*. It is in any case interesting to note that in the extensively revised edition of 1879/80 the subjective, individual, tragic ending was replaced by the characteristic reconciliation of the individual to society.

A further striking similarity between the *Bildungsroman* and the picaresque novel is the presence in both of a foster-father figure. Oskar Seidlin refers to this "mentor of old picaresque

---

[11]This and subsequent references to the works of Thomas Mann are to the *Stockholmer Gesamtausgabe der Werke von Thomas Mann* (Stockholm: Bermann-Fischer Verlag, 1939ff.), p. 1.

[12] Hermann Hesse, *Das Glasperlenspiel*, Vol. VI of *Gesammelte Schriften* (Berlin: Suhrkamp Verlag, 1952), p. 81. All subsequent references to the works of Hesse are to this edition.

[13]Victor Lange, "Stifter—Der Nachsommer," in *Der Deutsche Roman*, ed. Benno von Wiese (Düsseldorf: August Bagel Verlag, 1963), II, 49.

[14]Köhn, "Entwicklungs- und Bildungsroman," p. 441. Cf. Chapter 1, note 21.

literature," and traces his lineage back to the blind beggar in *Lazarillo de Tormes*, "who at the very beginning, promises the innocent and trusting little hero to initiate him into life."[15] At this point, however, it becomes more instructive to consider the contrasts between the two novel forms rather than the features they have in common. For if on a high level of abstraction the presence of a foster-father figure constitutes a point of contact for these two novel forms, in actuality the picaresque novel and the *Bildungsroman* are separate and distinct in their exploitation of this character.

The picaroon always encounters his mentor or foster-father figure early in the novel, often in the first chapter. His experience with this man is typically a sort of *déniaisement* or "wising-up," as Robert Alter describes it. [16] The archetypal situation for the picaresque novel is Lazarillo's encounter with the blind beggar, who opens the eyes of his young protégé to the ways of the world by slamming his head against a stone replica of a bull. In contrast, the hero of the *Bildungsroman* comes to terms with society only very gradually and often encounters his foster-father figure more toward the end of the novel.

The father figures themselves are studies in contrast. The mentor of the picaresque novel, like the picaroon himself, is an outsider who views cynically the relationship of the individual to society. His lesson for the young hero usually consists of rules for survival. He provides the young orphan with insights into the make-up of the world so that he may learn to outwit it.[17] The

---

[15]Seidlin, p. 174.

[16]Alter, pp. 30-31. The lesson that the picaroon must learn from his 'mentor' is basically that of sustaining and securing his person and personality in the face of an indifferent or even hostile world. In the archetypal picaresque novel, *Lazarillo de Tormes*, this struggle is reduced to its most basic terms. Lazarillo's story is the story of a daily battle against starvation.

[17]Alter, p. 3; cf. also p. 109.

typical foster father of the *Bildungsroman*, on the other hand, while he cannot deny a distant relationship to the outsider of the picaresque novel, is in fact a solid member of society. Although he, too, is concerned with the survival of the individual within the framework of a problematic social structure,[18] the main emphasis is placed upon the duties and responsibilities of the individual with respect to the whole.

The contrast that we observe between the figure of the mentor of the picaresque novel and the foster-father figure in the *Bildungsroman* corresponds to a basic, often documented contrast between the personalities of the picaroon and the hero of the German novel form. This contrast, as was indicated above, is usually formulated in terms of the lack of development and differentiation of the personality of the picaroon compared with the development of the "inner life," the *Bildung* of the hero of the *Bildungsroman*. It is perhaps more instructive, however, to consider another aspect of this contrast: The picaroon is fundamentally a realist and an empiricist—especially after his early encounter with the father figure, whereas the hero of the *Bildungsroman* is a dreamer and an idealist. The skeptical picaroon

---

[18] This aspect of the *Bildungsroman* is often overlooked by commentators who are restricted by a preconceived lexicographically conditioned definition of the genre. A closer look at the "Gesellschaft des Turmes" in *Wilhelm Meister* may make the comparison with the picaresque novel more convincing. Jarno tells Wilhelm: "Es ist gegenwärtig nichts weniger als rätlich, nur an einem Orte zu besitzen, nur einem Platze sein Geld anzuvertrauen, und es ist wieder schwer, an vielen Orten Aufsicht darüber zu fuhren; wir haben uns deswegen etwas anders ausgedacht: aus unserm alten Turm soll eine Sozietät ausgehen, die sich in alle Teile der Welt ausbreiten, in die man aus jedem Teile der Welt eintreten kann   *Wir assekurieren uns untereinander unsere Existenz*, auf den einzigen Fall, daß eine Staatsrevolution den einen oder den andern von seinen Besitztümern vertreibe." Pp. 563-64. (Italics mine).

has learned by experience to take very little for granted. In contrast, the hero of the *Bildungsroman*, if he is skeptical of anything at all, is skeptical of his own experience. As compared to the sudden *déniaisement* of the picaroon, his achievement of insight is slow, not always only because he is a "developing" character, but often also because his preconceived notion of the world, his idealism, is in conflict with his experience of the world. We need think only of Agathon before his meeting with Archytas or of the tenacity with which Wilhelm Meister clung to the illusion of his mission as an actor to visualize this contrast.

Paralleling the empiricism and skepticism of the picaroon, but contrasting with the idealism of the hero of the *Bildungsroman,* is a peculiar lack of vision on the part of the picaresque hero. The rogue can be ingeniously imaginative in extricating himself from one tight situation after another, but he exhibits a distinct and persistent lack of interest in changing the underlying situation which forces him to be continually on his guard, to have his wits continually about him. Robert Alter sees in this attitude a basic characteristic of the picaresque mentality. "The picaresque imagination is peculiarly an imagination that can make out nothing beyond the scope of the status quo. No matter how often the picaroon suffers . . . he never begins to imagine a different, more equitable society."[19] The contrast with the early representatives of the *Bildungsroman* is, of course, striking. Agathon and Wilhelm Meister are visionary characters par excellence. From the very beginning they are interested in nothing less than changing the make-up of the world, in reworking the fabric of society.

In the course of the novels Agathon and Wilhelm Meister learn what the picaroon seems to know instinctively, namely that in a confrontation between the world and the individual the world is overwhelmingly the more powerful. By reason of its sheer size and tremendous inertia the world has little trouble resisting the efforts

---

[19]Alter, p. 6.

of the individual to change it. The picaroon survives because he accepts the status quo, not as an insider, who might have something at stake in the established order, but as a pragmatic outsider who realizes that he must play by the rules if he is to play at all.[20] Both Agathon and Wilhelm Meister are exposed to a danger that the picaroon escapes by his acceptance of the status quo. Both incur the fundamental indifference and ultimately the enmity of the world they seek to transform. Both come dangerously close to surrendering their personal integrity. Wilhelm Meister, who would transform society with his art, finds his vehicle, the state, quickly and easily subverted by the demands of the public and the complicity of his fellow actors.[21] The warning from the ghost of Hamlet's father—"Zum ersten- und zum letzten mal! Flieh! Jüngling, flieh!"[22]—comes at the moment of greatest personal

---

[20]See Alter, p. 74: "If you do not play along with the people who set up the rules, you are likely to find that your life clashes with these rules, that these rules, the rule-makers, the whole world around you, grind on with relentless indifference or even enmity toward you and your integrity." The use of the word integrity here may surprise readers who are inclined to think of the picaroon only in terms of his roguery. Alter uses the word *integrity* in its primary meaning, which *Webster's New Twentieth Century Dictionary of the English Language,* unabridged 2nd edition ("The Publishers Guild, Inc." New York, 1965), p. 953 lists as "the quality or state of being complete; wholeness; entireness; unbroken state." The picaroon is an outsider, like Huckleberry Finn, who cannot accept an "insider" position in society without betraying his inner self, without sacrificing his personal integrity.

[21]While he was away visiting the Harfner, for example, "Melina scherzte nicht ganz fein über Wilhelms pedantische Ideale dieser Art, über Anmaßung, das Publikum zu bilden, statt sich von ihm bilden zu lassen, und beide vereinigten sich mit großer Überzeugung, daß man nur Geld einnehmen, reich werden oder sich lustig machen solle, und verbargen sich kaum, daß sie nur jener Personen los zu sein wünschten, die ihrem Plane im Wege standen." (*Wilhelm Meister*, p. 351).

[22] *Wilhelm Meister*, p. 328.

danger for Goethe's hero. The point had been reached when, if he stayed, Wilhelm would either be crushed by the indifference-born enmity of the troupe of actors or cease being Wilhelm Meister.

Agathon is in a similar situation at the court of Dionysius. After his disillusioning efforts to transform the state through the shaping of the personality of the ruler, he discovers that he has compromised his own ideals more than he has influenced the character of the tyrant. The envy, greed, and suspicion of the court, of the world at large, almost succeed in crushing him. Not only has he compromised his ideals, he has also lost much of his "enthusiasm," Wieland tells us,[23] and still he has met with no success in his world-changing endeavors. He is faced with the same alternative that confronts Wilhelm Meister: either he adopts the picaresque stance toward the world, either he becomes a "realist" who is willing to accept society for what it is, that is to say, either he ceases to be Agathon—or he will be crushed.[24]

In his moment of greatest personal peril, in the dungeon in Syracuse where he seriously considers for the first time the possibility of surrendering his personal integrity, of going over to the other side, Agathon, too, like Wilhelm Meister, receives a "warning" from a "ghost"—one from his past—in the person of Hippias. The unexpected reappearance of his former master shocks him to his sense: "Und sobald er in dem Manne, den er vor sich sah, den ganzen leibhaften Hippias, wie er ihn zu Smyrna verlassen hatte, wieder fand, fühlte er auch in sich wieder den

---

[23]*Agathon*, II, 387.
[24]Compare Wolfram Buddecke, *C. M. Wielands Entwicklungsbegriff und die Geschichte des Agathon,* (Palaestra: Untersuchen aus der deutschen und englischen Philologie und Literaturgeschichte), No, 235 (Göttingen: Vandenhoek & Ruprecht, 1966), p. 181: „Agathon hatte seine Anspruche nicht nur maßigen, sondern zurückziehen, er hatte sich selbst aufgeben und mit der Gemeinheit, die ihn vertrieb, paktieren müssen. Aber unter dieser Voraussetzung wäre ein Erfolg kein Erfolg gewesen; nicht Agathon hatte über die Welt, die Welt hätte über Agathon triumphiert."

ganzen Agathon."[25] But in Syracuse, as in Athens and Smyrna, being "Agathon" was not one of the alternatives that was open to him. He reads the warning clearly: "Flieh! Jüngling, flieh!" After the decision to retain his personal integrity, the only course open to him is the *deus ex machina* retreat to Tarent and Archytas.[26]

Up to this point the analysis has been purely descriptive, confined to a listing of formal and thematic similarities and contrasts between the two novel forms. We will now supplement our formal and thematic investigation by asking: What, leaving aside purely artistic or poetic considerations,[27] do the writers of picaresque novels and *Bildungsromane* seek to accomplish with

---

[25]*Agathon*, p. 430.

[26]The "flight" of Agathon to Tarent, like that of Wilhelm Meister to the *Turmgesellschaft*, seems to suggest that these "castles" or "quasi-islands" correspond to the "fluchtutopishe Insel" in Brunner's study. A decision on this question, however, must await a closer examination of the castle and the "castle experience" in each of these two novels.

[27]It is perhaps impossible to define rigidly the distinction between the purely poetic aspects and the non-poetic or extra-poetic aspects of a given literary work. Such a distinction can perhaps be intuited, however, by considering the extreme manifestations of the two possibilities. On the one hand would be works in the tradition of *l'art pour l'art*, on the other such patently non-poetic or pseudo-poetic literary works as didactic and philosophical tracts and political pamphlets. Keeping these two extremes in mind, I would hazard the following formulation: Purely poetic works or the purely poetic aspects of a given work speak directly and intimately to the individual and seek to establish in him a resonating re-creation or approximation of an original poetic experience or knowledge. Through the non-poetic aspect of a given work the author addresses himself to society at large, to man in general, and the subject of his discourse is the relationship of the reader to things and people outside the reader/author continuum.

We should remember here for future reference Brunner's distinction between the subjectively interpreted "poetic" islands and the non-poetic island of the social utopia.

their works? In the case of the picaresque novel, the extra-artistic intentions of the author are clearly in evidence. He is a social critic and a satirist. The picaroon is an excellent vehicle for his intentions. His position as an outsider who must learn the rules of a given society in order to survive provides an excellent perspective for viewing that society. [28] When society transgresses against the person of the picaroon, it usually does so in a manner which exposes its own inner inconsistencies and shortcomings. When, on the other hand, the picaroon transgresses against society, he does so on society's terms. He merely learns the unwritten rules followed by society and beats it at its own game—thereby effecting a further exposé of the shifting foundations and rotting superstructure of the social establishment. He is a "rogue" because he embodies in his person the inconsistencies of a society in a state of transition.[29] While paying lip service to "values and institutions whose strength was still officially proclaimed," [30] he bases his actions solely on the criterion of success.

---

[28]Wilfried van der Will—*Pikaro heute*, p. 8—considers the figure of the „outsider" itself an unspoken criticism of society: „Daß es sich um eine Außenseiterfigur handelt, wäre also nicht als Kritik gegen die Schriftsteller zu wenden, die eine solche Figur für ihre Erzählung gewählt haben, sondern ist als Kritik an einer Gesellschaft zu verstehen, in der Integrität, wenn überhaupt, so nur in der Randexistenz verwirklichbar wird." We note that Will, like Alter, stresses the importance of „integrity" to the picaroon. Were he a rogue just for the sake of being a rogue, that is, were it not a question of maintaining his personal integrity against the "relentless indifference or even enmity" of society, the figure of the picaroon would lose all deeper significance as a vehicle for social satire and social criticism.

[29] Compare Willy Schumann, "Wiederkehr der Schelme," *PMLA*, 81 (1966), 473-74: "Der Schelm ist im Grunde nur Widerspiegelung von Zeitumstanden. In ihm zeigt sich die Brüchigkeit und Fragwürdigkeit einer Epoche."

[30] See note 8 above.

The picaroon is frequently unaware of the inconsistency between his official belief and his actions. He is basically a problematical character.[31] But if the picaroon is not aware of this inconsistency, the reader is, and from this awareness proceeds with little difficulty to the awareness of the underlying inconsistencies in the society itself. By unmasking himself the picaroon unmasks the society behind him.

The fact that the social criticism implicit in the picaresque tradition is essentially negative has direct bearing on the question as to the respective extra-poetic intentions of the writers of picaresque novels and the writers of *Bildungsromane*. The picaresque novel exposes, ridicules, and condemns, but it does not offer an alternative to existing institutions or even indicate how the individual may relate himself positively, constructively to his imperfect, changing society. The inherently negative perspective of the picaresque situation is evident in a number of works which transcend the picaresque tradition. In *Candide*, Voltaire used the picaresque orphan figure as a vehicle for his stinging pessimistic social criticism. Unlike the traditional picaroon, however, but rather like the hero of the *Bildungsroman*, Candide retains his naïve idealism until shortly before the end.[32] The archetype of the modern novel, *Don Quixote*, likewise transcends the picaresque tradition without relinquishing the picaresque perspective. The heroes of these two novels are both consummate idealists, that is, they are essentially un-picaresque in their relationship to reality.

---

[31]See Alter, p. 4: "The fact that the Picaro can stand on a middle ground between the confidence of faith and the skepticism of irony is indicative of the peculiarly non-problematic attitude that the picaresque heroes take toward a distinctly problematical set of circumstances."

[32]Peter Gay—*The Enlightenment: An Interpretation. The Rise of Modern Paganism* (New York: Alfred A. Knopf, 1967), I, 199—argues that *Candide*, to the extent that it explodes the picaresque conventions, has become a *Bildungsroman*. His idea is certainly interesting, but suffers from an uncritical conception of the German novel form.

But they share with the more traditional picaresque hero an inability to survive—with their essential natures intact—as insiders and on the terms of their hypocritical society. Whereas the unproblematic picaroon survives by tacitly assuming the duplicity of society, by beating society at its own game, by wearing a mask or playing a role,[33] the idealistic hero, whose very nature, whose personal integrity involves a resisting of duplicity and a championing of the professed higher ideals and supposedly cherished institutions of his society, has no recourse but his own constancy, and is hence eventually broken by the untenable nature of his personal situation. It is first in the *Bildungsroman*, more specifically in Wieland's *Agathon*, that an attempt is made to offer a socially constructive answer to the dilemma of the individual caught up in the "picaresque situation."

That neither Agathon nor Wilhelm Meister is ultimately crushed by society, as were the idealists Don Quixote and Candide, does not refute the fact that both were placed in an inherently picaresque situation. The description of their life and the conflict between their ideals and their experience of reality up to the moment of crisis, when both receive the warning to flee, is the most convincing part of the two novels. A clear division separates the "realistic" bulk of these novels from the stylized final chapters.[34] To be completely convincing artistically, both novels

---

[33]Alter, p. 42, and Schumann, p. 473, stress this aspect of the picaroon's personality.

[34] Compare Georg Lukács, "Goethe und seine Zeit," in *Deutsche Literatur in zwei Jahrhunderten*, Vol. VII of *Werke* (Neuwied: Hermann Luchterhand Verlag, 1964), p. 84: „Seine Stilisierung besteht darin, daß er alle diese Tendenzen in der kleinen Gesellschaft des zweiten Teils konzentriert und diese konzentrierte Wirklichkeit der übrigen bürgerlichen Gesellschaft als eine Utopie gegenüberstellt." And Jürgen Jacobs, *Wielands Romane* (Bern: A. Francke Verlag, 1969), p. 65: „ . . . die Predigt des Archytas behauptet sich nicht gegen die dargestellte

should end tragically. In fact, however, extra-artistic con-siderations prevail. Wieland was not content with the negative criticism of the picaresque novel, with merely exposing, satirizing, tearing down, although satire is one of the most important elements of his art.[35] He intended to create in the figure of Agathon a useful example, a *utile exemplum* of responsible, moral conduct. A tragic resolution of the conflict would not be in keeping with the idea of the *utile exemplum*: Wieland, therefore, at the end attempts to portray positively the ideal relationship of the idealistic hero to an imperfect society.

Taken together—and interpreting revolution to mean a radical change in the institutions, practices and values of a society and/or in the thought and beliefs having a bearing on them—Seidlin's observation that the "scenery upon which the Picaro moves is an empire *on the eve of destruction* (emphasis added)"[36] and Pascal's remark that "all '*Bildungsromane*' were written in the *aftermath of revolution* (emphasis added) and social turmoil," [37] suggest a plausible partial explanation for the contrasting, complementary natures of *Bildungsromane* and picaresque novels with respect to the extra-poetic intentions of their authors. Both types of novel treat the plight of the individual in a complex, unsettled, changing society. The picaresque author's interest in satirically exposing and tearing down is consonant with a position in time before the collapse of an older order under the pressure of accumulated social and economic change. The *Bildungsroman* author's interest in constructing or at least in laying foundations, in stating the relationship of the hero to his society more positively, is consonant with a position later in time, after the collapse of the older order,

---

Wirklichkeit; sie wirkt dürr und gedanklich, und sie rettet wenig von dem Zauber der früher geschriebenen Teile."
[35]For example, one need mention only his *Geschichte der Abderiten*.
[36]See Note 8, above.
[37]See Note 7, above.

when building anew is of prime concern. Thus, the picaresque novel and the *Bildungsroman* appear to be allomorphic forms of a more general type of novel, one concerned with the relationship of the individual to a complex society in a state of flux, with the conditioning or determining factor being the author's sense of his position in time, that is, whether he interprets it as being before or after some critical turning point in the process of change. It is true that the subjective element involved in the poet's determining his position in time with regard to a radical change, a "revolution," may lead to a discrepancy between his and the more normal or the usual historical interpretation of his position in time, but also then, the poet with his intuition and imaginative insight may sometimes in a sense, even in a deeper sense, be correct.[38]

The work of Thomas Mann, who wrote both *Bildungsromane* and picaresque novels, offers an interesting corroboration for this theory. The original idea for *Felix Krull* occurred to Thomas Mann in the years preceding the collapse of the older order in World War I. The years following this holocaust saw him lay aside the satirical *Krull* in favor of his great *Bildungsroman, Der Zauberberg*. Years later, when the corruption and decadence in Western Civilization was once more uppermost in his mind, he returned to work on

---

[38]Thus Wieland, though he began his *Bildungsroman, Agathon*, some twenty years before the outbreak of the French Revolution, must have felt, owing to the destruction of his pietistic *Weltbild* by the thinking of the representatives of the French Enlightenment, that he was in effect living and writing *after* the collapse of the old order, after the "revolution." Samuel Clemens, on the other hand, though he wrote his picaresque *Huckleberry Finn* some twenty years after the supposed collapse of the old plantation order in the South, must have felt that the institutions and conventions of the pre-war slave states had not been seriously altered by the nominal abolishment of slavery and the defeat of the Confederacy in the Civil War, that this revolution had still to come.

Krull. In the works of several other writers similar corroborative evidence may be found.[39]

The plausibility of the thesis that the picaresque novel and the *Bildungsroman* are allomorphic representatives of a more general type also is enhanced by considerations of a sketch of the history of the two traditions. For the two centuries between the dates 1550 and 1750 the picaresque novel was cultivated in the literature of Spain, England and France.[40] The German contribution to the tradition during this epoch was nominal. The only significant picaresque novel written in Germany during this period, Grimmelshausen's *Simplicissimus*, is in fact a hybrid form, exhibiting features of both the picaresque novel and the *Bildungsroman*.[41] The temporary decline of the picaresque novel in

---

[39] The final version of *Agathon*, for example, written after the French Revolution, places a great deal more weight on the "positive" Archytas chapters than had been the case in the earlier versions. Hermann Hesse's *Steppenwolf* (1927), written in the waning days of the Twenties' boom, is the story not only of a man who harbors two personalities in his breast but the story of a man caught between two epochs, in a time, "in der Altes stirbt, ohne daß ein Neues geboren ist," [Herbert A. and Elisabeth Frenzel, *Daten deutscher Dichtung*, 3rd ed. (Köln und Berlin: Kiepenheuer & Witsch), 1962, p. 410.] Hesse's *Glasperlenspiel* (1943), written after the economic and social collapse of an older order in the thirties, states the relationship of the individual to society positively, in terms of the *Bildungsroman*.

[40] Alter, p. 104, uses these dates to describe the era when the picaresque novel was a "living genre."

[41] An *opinio communis*, with reference to which we began this investigation of the phenomenon *Bildungsroman*, would probably tend toward this statement as a compromise. Some writers, typified, perhaps, by Richard Alewyn, ["Erzählformen des deutschen Barock," *in Formkräfte der deutschen Dichtung* (Göttingen: Vandenhoek & Ruprecht, 1963), pp. 21-34], argue or assume that *Simplicissimus* is a picaresque novel, while others agree more or less with Melita Gerhard—*Der Deutsche Entwicklungsroman bis zu Goethes ‚Wilhelm Meister'* (Halle/Saale: Max

the middle of the eighteenth century heralds the rise of the *Bildungsroman* in Germany. Conversely, the apparent decline of the *Bildungsroman* in the twentieth century corresponds to a renewed interest in the picaresque novel.[42]

An explanation for this development would involve a discussion of the general sweep of European history during the past four hundred years as well as a more particular discussion of the rise and development of the art of the novel—and would thus exceed the bounds of this present investigation. A few remarks of a very general nature will, however, serve to indicate the direction that such an investigation might take.

The rise of the picaresque novel in sixteenth-century Spain corresponds not only to the decline and decay of the Spanish empire but to a tremendous rise in the social mobility of the middle class, caused by the influx of riches from the New World. Similar conditions did not exist in the lands of the Holy Roman Empire until much later. While Spain, and to an even larger extent, France and England, were evolving into modern centralized trading states, the Empire remained largely what it had been during the Middle Ages. Meanwhile the European novel was evolving in accordance with its own internal laws. By the eighteenth century, evolution within the picaresque tradition was moving toward the bursting of the basic

---

Niemeyer Verlag, 1926)—who views it in the narrower context of German literary tradition. The relationship of Grimmelshausen's great novel to the two novel traditions is a question deserving of more discussion than can be given within the context of the present work.

[42] Picaresque novels written after the middle of the eighteenth century tend, like Mark Twain's *Huckleberry Finn*, to be isolated from the mainstream of contemporary literature. The picaresque novel was sufficiently 'dead' during the century and a half before the year 1900—which roughly corresponds to the lifespan of the *Bildungsroman*—to warrant speaking of a 'revival' of the picaresque form in the twentieth century. Cf. R. W. Lewis, *The Picaresque Saint* (Philadelphia and New York: J. B. Lippincott Co., 1959), p. 10.

form. The central position of the picaresque hero tended to draw attention to his individual, spiritual and psychological development.[43] The simple structure of the picaresque novel with its emphasis on adventure and external events did not seem adequate—especially after the appearance of Rousseau's *Nouvelle Héloïse* in 1761—for the exposition of the inner life of a complex character. The decline of the picaresque form in the middle of the eighteenth century coincides thus with the rise of the psychological novel.[44] Paralleling the growing psychological complexity of the typical novel hero in the middle of the eighteenth century is a trend away from the simplistic satirical critical description of society presented by the picaresque novel toward a more objective critical analysis of society and man's relation to it. This tendency, observable in the novels of Daniel Defoe, led in the late eighteenth and in the nineteenth century to the *Gesellschaftsroman* or the *Zeitroman*.

The first *Bildungsromane* may be thought of as the work of men who were intellectually the product of the late eighteenth century but emotionally on a par with other Western Europeans of an earlier age. Their emotional—and real—experience of the world was that of one in a state of obsolescence and disintegration. Germany in the late eighteenth century was in the early stages of a political, social and economic upheaval that had essentially run its course in her neighbors to the west. Intellectually, however, these men viewed the world from the vantage point of a late eighteenth-century "enlightened" European. The basically picaresque form of the *Bildungsroman* and the underlying concern with the relationship of the individual to a society experiencing the

---

[43] Compare Alter, p. 32: ". . . it was a natural temptation for the author to begin concerning himself with the individual personality of this real individual at the center of the episodic narrative."

[44] See Wilpert's discussion of the "psychologischer Roman," *Sachwörterbuch*, p. 546.

transformation from a feudal, land-based economy to a bourgeois economy based on trade and industry testifies to their emotional kinship with the earlier picaresque authors in Spain, France, and England. The greater interest in the psychological development of the hero, the increased objectivity with which they analyzed social institutions, and the will to work out a mutually fruitful relationship between the individual and society testify to their acquaintance with the streams of contemporary European thought.

The *Bildungsroman* is thus the hybrid product of two epochs in European history.[45] The coincidence in Germany of these two epochs—the earlier socio-economic-politico-emotional and the contemporary intellectual—gives rise to a type of novel which exhibits characteristics observable only separately in other European literatures. In the *Bildungsroman* the emotionally conditioned, simplistic picaresque structure is called upon to support the intellectually conditioned content of the psychological novel and the *Zeit-* or *Gesellschaftsroman*. The *Bildungsroman* is thus the extension and development of the picaresque novel, under the special German conditions, past the point where it may be considered picaresque.

The peculiar hybrid nature of the *Bildungsroman* is, of course, the very reason why so many scholars have been confused as to its essential nature. Many writers, noting that Wieland has referred to *Agathon* as a Seelen-Geschichte, are content to consider this novel under the rubric *psychologischer Roman.* Other writers have been tempted by the epic breadth of *Wilhelm Meister* to call it a *Zeitroman*.[46] Most novels that have been termed *Bildungsromane*

---

[45]Lucács, *Deutsche Literatur in zwei Jahrhunderten,* p. 377, accounts for the popularity of the novella in Germany by referring to the peculiar, anachronistic quality of German society.

[46] See Köhn, p. 439: "Als Beispiele nennt Kayser ... die Zeit- und Gesellschaftsromane des 19. Jahrhunderts, aber—und das ist nicht unwichtig—auch die ‚Lehrjahre' mochte er in diesem Zusammenhang sehen."

lend themselves likewise to interpretation under one or the other of these two general headings, depending upon whether the *psycho*-analytical or *social*-analytical aspect receives the relatively greater stress. *Der Grüne Heinrich*, for instance, with its emphasis on the hero's childhood experiences, is often considered a psychological novel.[47] *Der Zauberberg*, on the other hand, is often considered to be one of the great *Zeitromane* of the twentieth century.

In the famous "crisis of the novel" in the twentieth century the traditional novel forms of the eighteenth and nineteenth centuries seem to lose their validity. The psycho- and socio-analytic tools of the traditional novel no longer seem adequate for the description of a dramatically different and quickly changing reality. As the *Bildungsroman* is stripped of the historically conditioned elements, it once again bares its essential structure. We recognize once more the picaresque novel, with its pressing central question concerning the relationship of the individual to an incompatible, ruthless, and complex society in a state of flux.

---

[47] For example, Wilpert, p. 546.

CHAPTER 3: A NEW TRADITION

I n *Agathon*, with which the history of the modern German novel, of the *Bildungsroman*, may be said to begin, we find Wieland struggling with the great unassimilated legacy of the seventeenth century. The theme of *vanitas vanitatum* is intoned in the opening paragraphs of the first chapter.[1] The ever-present problem for the seventeenth-century hero, the seemingly irreconcilable conflict between man's spiritual and animal natures, is recast here in the sentimental terms of "Kopf" and "Herz."[2] In *Agathon*, as in the heroic or courtly baroque novel, the constancy of the moral hero is tested and proves itself against the inconstancy of the world about him.

Two major European novel traditions converge in this first important German novel of the eighteenth century: The Iberian-born picaresque novel is wedded to the courtly novel—satirized by Cervantes in *Don Quixote*—it also of Spanish-Portuguese origin.[3]

---

[1] Friedrich Senle, *Christoph Martin Wieland* (Stuttgart: Metzlersche Verlagsbuchhandlung, 1949), pp. 85-86, notes: „Wielands heitere Lebenslehre ist stets nur das ideelle Gegengewicht gegen den ‚Pessimismus' eines tieferen Seins: das Vanitas vanitatum-Motiv klingt noch erstaunlich stark in ihm."

[2] This conflict is actually many-sided and complicated in *Agathon*. We might expect that Wieland, as an *Aufklärer*, would tend to give precedence to "Kopf." As will become clearer in the course of this discussion, however, in each important crisis it is the "Herz" which emerges triumphant, leaving the "Kopf" to accommodate itself as best it can to the sovereign dicta.

[3] Alewyn, „Erzählformen," p. 22, views the baroque novel in terms of these two European novel traditions: "Nur mit der Gattung Barockroman haben wir es hier zu tun, nicht mit ihren individuellen Variationen, oder vielmehr mit den zwei Gattungen, die fast unbeschränkt im 17

The picaresque novel, as we have noted, is the novel of the outsider, presenting a negative picture of society from his vantage point. The courtly novel, on the other hand—and here I use the term broadly with Alewyn to include the many seventeenth-century manifestations, such as *heroischer Roman, heroisch-galanter Roman*, and *Staatsroman*—is the novel of the insider.[4] As all the various designations of this genre suggest, we are not confronted here with rejected, "low" characters, but with society's chosen few, with princes and princesses, with knights and fair, noble maidens. In the courtly novel the implications of society's official beliefs, both religious and secular, are explored and affirmed. The hero of the courtly novel is an exemplary character whose experience and actions embody the beliefs and ideals of his society.

Agathon is basically the story of the idealistic "insider" hero of the courtly novel placed in the "outsider," picaresque situation.[5] He will be called upon to prove himself (*sich bewähren*), as are the protagonists of the heroic novel, but his trial will be infinitely more arduous than that of the seventeenth-century hero. Whereas the typical baroque hero has a firm frame of reference to guide him in

---

Jahrhundert das Feld des Romans beherrschten: dem Picaro-roman (oder Schelmenroman) und dem Heroischen Roman, auch Heroisch-Galanter Roman oder Höfischer Roman, oder Staatsroman genannt."

[4]Ibid.

[5]This rather abstract, simplistic conception of Wieland's novel should be understood as a complement to the equally abstract formulation, developed at the end of the preceding section, which considers *Agathon*, as the first *Bildungsroman*, the sum of the emotionally conditioned moment of socio- and psycho-analysis. Any such single, simple statement can naturally describe only part of the whole truth, which is plural and complex. We should note, however, that Agathon's "insider" position corresponds to the more positive thrust of the *Bildungsroman* compared to the picaresque novel.

his moral choices and actions, Agathon's experience of the world, like that of all true picaresque heroes, seems to open to question the very basis for the accepted moral code.[6] His trial involves not the mere preservation of his moral self in the face of the temptations and distractions of the world, but the preservation of his belief in the possibility of a moral order altogether.

The differences between the idealistic, moral hero of the seventeenth century—whether he be the hero of a courtly novel or Simplicissimus at the end of his wandering—and Agathon, reflect, of course, one of the fundamental differences between the seventeenth and the eighteenth century: The former was primarily "other-worldly," whereas the latter, the age of the Enlightenment, was predominantly "this-worldly." In the Middle Ages it had been possible for the individual to serve both God and society, which was divinely established. As the old order, despite its divine origin, began to disintegrate with the rise of capitalism, the national state, and the discovery of the New World at the close of the Middle Ages, many moralists began to shift the emphasis even further away from the world and place it more and more exclusively on the service to God. The state of social flux which gradually became obvious, and has continued to be characteristic of Europe since the dawn of the Renaissance, was all too often viewed not as a crisis for society but as one for the individual, who was now felt to be adrift in a world almost completely divorced from God. The primary task for a moral man accordingly became the salvation of his own immortal soul. If circumstances seemed to warrant it—and in the seventeenth century, when this sentiment was at a peak, they seemed to do just that—the moral man was justified in turning his back on society for the single purpose of saving his soul.

---

[6]Melitta Gerhard, p. 107, remarks: „Zwischen Recht und Unrecht kann Simplicius wählen, was Recht und Unrecht ist, ist das Problem des ‚Agathon.'"

Such an alternative was not acceptable to the moralists of the Enlightenment, with their radically different mode of thinking. The crowning idea of the Enlightenment, the belief in human progress,[7] had taken shape under the influence of the humanism of the Renaissance and the tremendous scientific and technological advances of the seventeenth century. A man imbued with this belief could not retreat with good conscience from the struggle for mankind in order to concern himself with purely personal salvation—even if the traditional Christian sense of virtue and morality seemed to counsel such a retreat. This situation was actually further complicated by the fact that uncertainty about Christianity and the nature of God, until then the ultimate court of decision in moral questions, began to disturb many thoughtful men.

This uncertainty was all the more disturbing because of its ready visibility in society. The eighteenth century witnessed a great increase in the number and activity of the conflicting sects within Christianity, as well as an intensification of the attacks from without. The skill of these attacks frequently seemed to rob Christianity of its existential basis, while the nature of the tactics used to shore up Christianity against them frequently seemed to rob it of its essence, leaving behind for those accustomed to an established moral code an uncomfortable moral vacuum. Rushing into this vacuum came skeptical empiricists and materialists, who

---

[7] Robert Shackleton writes in "French Literature: The 18th Century," *Encyclopediae Britannica*, 1968, IX, 895: "The belief in progress is found in most philosophical works of this period; . . . it received its final expression in a work which sums up the aspirations of the 18th century, the *Esquisse d'un tableau historique des progrès de l'esprit humain* (1795) of Antoine Nicolas de Condorcet."

sought to replace the Christian concern with spiritual salvation in another world with this-worldly hedonism.[8]

To combat such a "selfish" doctrine, and to remove the emotional drain of moral uncertainty, a great number of thinkers in the eighteenth century, including Wieland, began to search for a new basis for a more socially oriented conception of morality, one that would be more in keeping with the spirit or essence of Christianity, with the "love thy neighbor" of the New Testament. Many intuited or sought to discover a link between the crowning idea of the age—the idea of progress—and the more altruistic elements of Christian teaching. For them the Good Samaritan of the parable became the *Weltverbesserer*, called upon not just to exercise Christian charity, but to right the wrongs, soothe the ills, and bind up the wounds of a whole generation. For these children of the Enlightenment, the New Testament imperative became "love mankind."

Thus in the eighteenth century a new faith, a new idealism, a new belief—ill-founded as it might seem at times—in the basic goodness, educability, and perfectibility of man gradually replaces the older belief in sinful, fallen man in need of redemption. The eighteenth-century thinkers were, of course, no more successful in establishing rigorous philosophic or scientific proofs for their belief in progress than the medieval scholastics were in proving the existence of God. This new Weltanschauung, in its myriad forms, was essentially an article of faith, accepted by enough of the prominent thinkers of the age to give the eighteenth century its characteristic optimistic cast.

That the belief in progress was never to secure for itself the same legitimacy that had been enjoyed by the older faith during

---

[8] The unconvincing Anacreontic poetry of mid-eighteenth-century Germany is a monument to the moral and emotional uncertainty of these latter-day pagans.

the Middle Ages was due to a plurality of causes. Conservative thinkers among the clergy, who were naturally suspicious of the this-worldly tendency of a belief in human progress, continued to exercise great power. The rise of Rousseau's cultural pessimism after the middle of the century provided an even greater challenge to the basic tenets of this new faith. The most serious threat to a belief in human progress came, however, not from theologians and philosophers, but from the experience of the world itself. Human greed seemed to acquire a new dimension in the eighteenth century with the birth of modern speculative capitalism. To an observer such as Voltaire, the senseless slaughter of the Seven Years' War marked no significant advance in human aspirations and human behavior. The atrocities and the endless conflicts and wars of the French Revolution, which had been hailed by many as a great victory for humanity and the greatest milestone in the history of human progress, soon disillusioned all but its most determined supporters. Wieland himself often derided the popular contention that his age was any more "enlightened" or significantly more advanced than any other epoch in recorded history.[9]

In *Agathon* the representative of this new idealism is forced to come to terms with the realities of eighteenth-century life. Agathon, the exemplary insider of the courtly novel, is here afforded the rogue's *outsider* view and experience of society. As we have noted, Wieland's extra-literary considerations make a realistic tragic ending unacceptable to him. His *Agathon*, the first *Bildungsroman*, may be regarded as a search for alternatives.

****

---

[9]Gay, II, 107

The first alternative that Wieland considers—albeit only rhetorically—is the classical picaresque solution to the conflict between the individual and society. After we have been introduced to Agathon in Book 1 and have learned something of his life as the shuttlecock of Fortune, our hero temporarily ends his wanderings as the slave of Hippias in Smyrna. By assuming the position of slave or servant, Agathon fulfills the traditional role assigned to the picaroon from Lazarillo de Tormes in the sixteenth century to Gil Blas in the eighteenth and to Felix Krull in the twentieth.[10] Although an outsider, the servant or slave is often privy to the behind-the-scenes activities of the ruling social class. He has the opportunity to peer behind the façade. This opportunity is afforded to Agathon to an unusual degree. His master, Hippias, is not only a perfect example of the duplicity of character which is the subject of exposé in the traditional picaresque novel—he has made a science of his duplicity and seeks to win Agathon as his star pupil and disciple.

The figure of Hippias corresponds, of course, to the mentor of the picaresque novel. Not only does he appear near the beginning of the novel, as do the traditional mentor figures in the picaresque tradition: Hippias propounds the characteristic picaresque form of wisdom. He proposes to introduce Agathon into the ways of the world. Hippias does know the world, as Agathon is ready to admit at the end of the novel,[11] but the use to which he puts this knowledge is unacceptable to the idealistic hero. Since he cannot

---

[10]Alter, p. 15, notes: "In connection with the inherent satirical perspective of the picaresque situation, it is especially significant that the picaroon is a servant of many masters."

[11]*Agathon*, p. 575: „Seine Beobachtungen . . . überzeugten ihn, daß die Menschen, im Durchschnitt genommen, überall so sind, wie Hippias sie schilderte."

accept the cynical conclusions drawn by Hippias, Agathon long refuses to see the basic accuracy of his observations.

Agathon was actually much more knowledgeable in the ways of the world than Hippias had reason to suspect when he purchased him from the Sicilian pirates. After his experiences in Athens we might expect him to be very receptive to the ideas of the sophist. Looking back on those days he later tells Danae: "Alles, womit Ich . . . mein Unglück . . . verdient . . . ist Unvorsichtigkeit, oder Mangel an derjenigen Klugheit, welche nur die Erfahrung geben kann."[12] This *Klugheit,* this lesser form of wisdom, is precisely the science that Hippias teaches. Why does Agathon then so steadfastly resist Hippias' teaching? The obvious answer—that Agathon is virtuous, whereas Hippias is an immoral man—does not get to the heart of the matter. On the whole, the figure of the sophist is presented quite positively in the novel. Hippias is shown to be an eminently reasonable man who exhibits genuine fatherly concern for the welfare of the young dreamer. The answer to this central question involves a review of Agathon's (and Wieland's) views on morality.

Just as Agathon, if he is not a charlatan, seems to Hippias to be "eine lebendige Widerlegung meines Systems,"[13] so the sophists' cynical doctrine, if it be true, seems to Agathon to rob men of the basis for moral action. For although it is nowhere stated explicitly, it is clear from his actions that Agathon has all along adopted a pragmatist's rationale for virtue. He sets out in Athens, and then more determinedly in Syracuse, to show *Quid Virtus et quid Sapientia possit.* When he fails in both attempts to produce any tangible results—except suffering for himself—his faith in the power of virtue is profoundly shaken.

---

[12] *Agathon,* p. 246.
[13] *Agathon,* p. 113.

It seems that Wieland himself was not quite sure how he should think on this point. Like many eighteenth-century thinkers, missing the traditional theological basis for virtue and moral action, Wieland felt compelled to posit some reasonable, practical basis for it. Being a rather genial but by no means profound or rigorous thinker, Wieland began with a somewhat vague, traditional notion of *Tugend*, and then set himself the task of demonstrating that it was good for the world. He was immediately placed on the defensive by cynical skeptics such as Hippias. His more famous and infinitely more profound contemporary, Immanuel Kant, drawing on a religious and emotional background quite similar to that of Wieland, asserted the basis for a traditional[14] conception of virtue and moral action philosophically. His categorical imperative simply enjoins the moral man to act only upon the maxim which he can will at the same time to become a universal law. A man such as Hippias, who cannot wish that his personal maxims, his "system," attain the status of universal law, cannot shake the foundation of the rigorous Kantian ethics. He is contained within the system of Kantian thought as a base or immoral man. To Wieland, the student of Shaftesbury, to whom every type of system was foolish, no such philosophical certainty was possible.[15]

The non-systematic thought of the optimistic cosmopolites, Shaftesbury and Wieland, lent itself readily to experimental verification—but also to apparent refutation. With his doctrine of

---

[14] "Traditional" in the sense that it does not contradict the spirit of Christianity. His categorical imperative is little more than a philosophically rigorous "golden rule." An example of a "non-traditional" conception of virtue or morality might be given by a cynical materialist who argues that "might makes right."

[15] Anthony Earl of Shaftesbury, "Advice to an Author," in *Characteristics*, ed. John M. Robertson (Gloucester, Mass.: Peter Smith, 1963), I, 189: "The most ingenious way of becoming foolish is by a system." See also Jacobs, *Wieland*, p. 37.

natural affections Shaftesbury had sought to remove the theoretical basis for the hypothetical, selfish creations of Locke and
Hobbes.[16] Shaftesbury had contended that the selfish individuals
postulated by the English philosophers need merely to be taught
how to be "rightly selfish" in order to be transformed into model
citizens.[17] True wisdom, as contrasted with the specious reasoning
of the sophists, would lead necessarily to a love of virtue. According to this line of thinking a virtuous man such as Agathon needs
merely to "enlighten" a profligate tyrant such as Dionysius with
regard to the manifold advantages of virtue to transform him into
the most exemplary philosopher-king. The events in Syracuse
seemed to provide a convincing experimental refutation of this
theory.

If Agathon's love of virtue had been based completely on
reasoning such as Shaftesbury's, he would have been forced at this
point to concede victory to Hippias and join forces with the cynic
against the world. In his heart, however, Agathon felt no need to
rationalize virtue. The sudden reappearance of Hippias in Syracuse,
as we have noted, shocks him into his senses with regard to the
nature of the world and the nature of the conflict in his own breast.
Although the world is indeed as Hippias describes it, Agathon,
somewhat to his own surprise, discovers that it is not therefore
necessary to assume the picaresque stance with respect to it that
the sophist recommends. Although Agathon may not find it
possible to effect sweeping changes in the make-up of society, it
does not follow necessarily that he must turn his back on society's
problems and seek—as Hippias—to turn its weaknesses to his
personal advantage. In effect, Agathon has approached the moral

---

[16]Shaftesbury, "On the Freedom of Wit and Humour," in *Characteristics*,
I, 63, and 77-78.
[17]Shaftesbury, "On the Freedom," p. 81.

position of Kant, who speaks not so much of the advantages that may be gained by moral action, as of duty.

Reference to duty in a literary work usually carries the hidden implication of tragedy. Robert Alter reminds us that for Don Quixote life was the fulfillment of a duty, both to himself and to the world.[18] The alternative to the tragic ending of *Don Quixote* that Wieland explores in *Agathon* sets his novel apart from the other novels that had grown out of the older picaresque tradition. It is a formula which has been adopted by all subsequent *Bildungs-romane*. Agathon is not forced to choose between becoming an *outsider* or being eliminated or destroyed by society. He is enabled to preserve his personal integrity and to discharge his moral duty to society. Agathon's flight to Tarent and Archytas is not a flight away from his responsibilities as a citizen and as an *Aufklärer*, but a retreat from an untenable position. Agathon will continue to fight the good fight, though he can no longer look for a quick and easy victory. His immediate activities will in fact be of a distinctly defensive nature.

****

In *Die Geschichte des weisen Danishmend* (1775) Wieland had explored the *fluchtutopische* solution to the dilemma in which Agathon finds himself after the Syracuse episode. Danishmend, like Agathon, incurs the displeasure of a tyrant and must flee. Although he is convinced of the incorrigibility of society,[19] he, like Agathon, rejects the attitude of the cynic Kalender/Hippias who preys on the weakness of society for personal gain. The disillusioned Danishmend, having found an ideal of absolute value in the joy of

---

[18]Alter, p. 109.

[19] Sengle, p. 281, "Danishmend ist so gut wie der Kalender daran verzweifelt, die Welt im großen bessern zu können."

familial harmony, abandons his calling as social *Wundarzt* and devotes himself to his family and to its protection in the idyllic seclusion of a retreat from the world.[20] But this is not Wieland's solution in *Agathon*. The relationship that Agathon must learn to assume with respect to society is one of a peculiar ambivalence. If he is to survive, he must insulate himself to a certain extent from the dangers of social life. If he isolates himself completely from society, however, as does Danishmend, he shirks his responsibility as a moral man to work for the improvement of society. Agathon must learn somehow to protect himself from society without forfeiting the possibility of effecting changes within that society. Agathon must be both a refugee from society and a social reformer. He must be able to immerse himself in society without submerging in the tidal wash of powerful social currents and political upheavals. He must retain the ability to function in an imperfect society without surrendering his personal integrity to the demands placed upon him by that society. He must first secure for himself a position of relative stability within the shifting cross-currents of social life, and then, from this position of relative strength and security, begin, cautiously at first, the never-ending task of social reform. Quixotic knight-errantry—that is, any attempt at a dramatic single-handed righting of social wrongs, such as Agathon undertook in Athens and later in Syracuse—will end in disillusionment and tragedy.

The ideal relationship of the moral hero to his imperfect society is discovered to Agathon in the person and life of Archytas, in whom Wieland gives Agathon a second mentor—this time a true

---

[20]Sengle, p. 282, „Aber eine Gemeinschaftsform, die bisher in Wielands Schriften überhaupt nicht ins Blickfeld trat, ist ihm zu einem unzweifelhaften Werte geworden: die Familie . . . Wieland hat der Rolle eines Menschheitsbeglückers entsagt. Er überläßt den Sultanen willig die Welt, wenn sie ihm nur seinen kleinen Kreis nicht zerstören wollen."

spiritual kin and foster father. „Der Weise Archytas," in contrast to Danishmend, though equally concerned with the preservation of his family in the face of constant dangers from without, retains a keen sense of his moral duty to help improve the lot and the moral stature of his fellow man. Far from separating himself from the fate of his country, he continues to concern himself intimately with the welfare of the little republic. For more than thirty years Archytas has been the most conscientious and most respected public servant in Tarent. During this time, however, he has remained serenely aloof from the political infighting that had jeopardized Agathon's career in Athens and in Syracuse. Archytas owes his success in Tarent, not to the political skills of oration and manipulation, but to his ability to lead his people through the power of his own exemplary life and actions. Speaking of the family of the wise Archytas, Dane tells Agathon: „Nur eine einzige Familie, wie diese worin du jetzt lebst . . . an jedem Orte, wo Menschen wohnen . . . Plato selbst würde keine Gesetze erfinden können, welche mehr Gutes wirkten, als ein solches *Beispiel* der Tugend und der Glückseligkeit."[21] (Italics mine)

At the writing of the final version of *Agathon* Wieland envisions thus a wider role for the family than in *Danishmend*. It now serves as the middle link between the individual and society. The family offers Agathon the proper balance of contact with and isolation from society that up until his arrival in Tarent had escaped him. As the smallest, self-contained structured unit of society the family is ideally suited to the double task of providing a haven for the individual and of serving as an exemplary microcosmic model for the larger society.[22]

---

[21]*Agathon*, p. 539.

[22] For Wieland, as for many German *Aufklärer*, who tempered their republican idealism with a healthy distrust of the masses, the ideal form of social organization was that of a benevolent patriarchy. The family,

In contrast with the ambitious reforms that Agathon had attempted to introduce in Athens and Syracuse, the program that is outlined here is modest indeed. Wieland does not hesitate to point out that the substantial successes enjoyed by Archytas in Tarent are due in a large measure to a series of fortunate coincidences.[23] The program has in fact been brought into line with the realities of the marketplace. Utopia is not around the corner, to be reached by a few quick strokes of the magic wand of *Tugend*. The difficulty, of course, is that a man already hardened by his experience of the world is not inclined to allow this education to

---

particularly the patriarchal family of the eighteenth-century *Bürgertum*, was thus the ideal proving ground for his social theories. Agathon had argued for a patriarchal form of government in Syracuse—„Denn Agathon hatte nicht die Tyrannei, sondern die Regierung eines Vaters angepriesen, der seine Kinder wohl erzieht und glücklich zu machen sucht" (*Agathon*, p. 378)—but just because his ideas had such popular appeal was Agathon destined to failure. On the one hand Agathon's popularity aroused the suspicion and jealousy of professional politicians. On the other hand, the people, "die Menge," always at the mercy of "Wortkünstler" and "überedner" such as Hippias, were shown to be a very fickle ally.

[23] Archytas, for example, owes his serenity and wisdom partly to an essentially negative aspect of his personality. "Archytas hatte niemals weder eine glühende Einbildungskraft noch heftige Leidenschaften gehabt . . . [es kostete] . . . ihm wenig Mühe, Ruhe und Ordnung in seiner innerlichen Verfassung zu erhalten," (*Agathon*, p. 456f.) Wieland describes the happy republic as being „zu klein, um ehrgeizige Entwürfe zu machen; zu groß, um den Ehrgeiz und die Vergrößerungssucht ihrer Nachbarn fürchten zu müssen; zu schwach, um in andern Unternehmungen als in den Künsten des Friedens ihren Vorteil zu finden; aber stark genug, sich gegen jeden nicht allzu übermächtigen Feind (und einen solchen hatte sie damals noch nicht) in ihrer Verfassung zu erhalten." (*Agathon*, p. 453).

begin with himself.[24] He is not interested in social experiments, at least not for himself, but he may be won by example, as Archytas' success, under favorable circumstances, demonstrates. To a certain extent, then, Agathon's faith in the power of virtue is vindicated, even as Hippias' skepticism is shown to be well-founded. While the world does not suffer patiently the incessant probing and prodding of idealistic reformers, neither is the individual citizen of the world completely immune to the salubrious effects of good example. Men such as Agathon may not discharge their duty with respect to society by undertaking the heroic but fruitless task of reversing the tide of current events. Like his humble brother, the picaroon, the hero of the first *Bildungsroman*, while not an anti-hero, must learn to be unheroic. He must resist engaging the enemy on its own terms and own terrain, for the enemy's strength is too great, and Agathon's cause too important for the risk of defeat. Agathon must survive—that was the primary task of the picaroon—so that his exemplary life may become a beacon and a promise of a better world to come.

The necessity of the retreat to the relative isolation and security of the family is occasioned not only by the real threats to the hero's physical well-being: in periods of transition the individual tends to become confused as to the validity of his own ideals, which are culturally conditioned. As society's conventions gradually lose their validity, the foundation of an individual's faith becomes increasingly subjective.[25] A man such as Agathon, who

---

[24]*Agathon*, p. 576.

[25]Sengle, p. 195, writes: „Wo die objektive Welt mit ihren Ordnungen oder wenigstens Konventionen keine Gültigkeit mehr hatte, mußte die Frage der (subjektiven) *Weltanschauung* eine große Dringlichkeit gewinnen. In der Geschichte der deutschen Dichtung bezeichnet *Agathon* diesen Übergang am augenfälligsten."

bears the proof of his idealistic faith in his own heart, but who is continually confronted with contradictory evidence from without, may be brought dangerously close to disaster as long as heart or feeling are his only guide.[26] If he is to survive, the idealist must have some retreat in which he can collect his thoughts,[27] in which he can through study and contemplation seek some objective substantiation for his belief, and in which he can—it is hoped—observe and enjoy the fruits of his idealistic endeavors.

We may now answer—at least with respect to *Agathon*—the question we raised in Chapter 1 as to the thematic and formal role of the foster-father figure in the *Bildungsroman*. The figure of Archytas is necessary—both thematically, as a counterpoise to the figure of Hippias, and formally, as a *deus ex machina* solution to a

---

[26]*Agathon*, p. 426: „Es kamen Augenblicke, wo er . . . geneigt schien, sich selbst von der Wahrheit der Hippiassischen Theorie zu überreden." Later (p. 544), he tells Archytas: „Mein Herz blieb zwar noch immer mein einziger Führer; aber auch dieses geriet durch allzu große Sicherheit in Gefahr, sich selbst zu täuschen."

[27]One of Agathon's principal tasks is the reconciliation of his *Herz* with his *Kopf*. (See note 2 above) Wieland reminds the reader that for such a task peace and quiet are necessary. „Seine Vernunft konnte in diesem Stucke mit seinem Herzen, und sein Herz mich sich selbst nicht recht einig werden: und er war nicht ruhig genug, seine nunmehrigen Begriffe in ein System zu bringen, wodurch beide hatte befriedigt werden können. In der Tat ist ein Schiff eben nicht der bequemste Ort, ein solches Werk, wozu die Stille eines dunkeln Hains kaum stille genug ist, zu Stande zu bringen." (*Agathon*, p. 305) In Tarent, then, under the guidance of Archytas, Agathon enters upon a strenuous program of study to cultivate his mind to a degree that it may become the worthy and helpful partner of his heart. It remains, however, one of the fatal weaknesses of the novel, at least from an artistic point of view, that just what it is that Agathon learns under Archytas' tutelage beyond the picaresque wisdom—that he must not confront the world directly if he is to remain Agathon—is left uncomfortably vague.

hopeless dilemma—for the reconciliation of Agathon to society. It is not unreasonable to say that the tradition of the German *Bildungsroman* begins with the figure of Archytas, who replaces—we see it happen in the novel—the cynical, selfish mentor of the picaresque tradition. The figure of Archytas corresponds to the positive moment of the *Bildungsroman*. If Agathon learns from Hippias and his own experience of the seemingly hopeless duplicity of society, he learns from the example of Archytas how he may protect himself from that society without fleeing from it. Just as the mentor in the picaresque novel presents through teaching and example a model for survival in a problematical social milieu, the foster father of the *Bildungsroman* —in *Agathon*, at least—presents a model for moral citizenship in a not too different world.

****

It should be clear from the foregoing that neither of the two main types of poetic islands abstracted by Brunner could adequately symbolize the ambivalent relationship of the moral individual to society proposed by the first *Bildungsroman*. A certain type of quasi-island, however, namely the castle, is capable of meeting the artistic needs of the *Bildungsroman*. While the castle is sufficiently island-like to suggest the problematical in the relationship of the individual to his society, since it is not really an island, since its isolation is not absolute, it may symbolize the peculiar relationship of the hero of the *Bildungsroman* to the world. The castle may signify a refuge and a retreat from society, but also a formative force, a focal point for developments within that society. The castle may serve as the symbol of the fulfilment of the moral individual's double responsibility: toward himself and the conservation of his personal integrity, and toward society, for the improvement of which he must constantly work.

In *Agathon* the house or villa of *Der Weise Archytas* performs the functions ascribed above to the castle in the *Bildungsroman*.[28] Because Archytas has, through long years of study and service, succeeded already before Agathon's arrival in transforming the city-state of Tarent to the point that it represents an exception to the general picture of society presented in the novel, the negative function of the castle, that of protecting its inhabitants from harmful influences from without, is no longer of paramount importance and no longer stressed. Archytas' house is thus not very castle-like; it is in no sense a parapeted fortress sustaining daily attacks. To be sure, it still represents a refuge and asylum for Agathon, but its positive function as a microcosmic model of social harmony receives the greater emphasis. The house of Archytas is a living realization of that ineffable ideal of social harmony toward which the little republic of Tarent continually strives. Wieland describes the effect it has on Agathon thus:

---

[28] Much of what in later years is easily recognizable as an important element in a literary tradition may be present in the early representatives of such a tradition in embryonic, undifferentiated form. The present analysis of the role of the castle in the first example of the *Bildungsroman* would probably not have suggested itself without some acquaintance with the role of the castle in the subsequent novels in the tradition. As we shall see in the next chapter, the elaborate, consciously artistic use that Goethe makes of this versatile literary device contrasts markedly with the casual, almost accidental use Wieland makes of it. This analysis would likewise not have been possible without a fresh appraisal of what is meant by the term *Bildungsroman*, an appraisal which was in turn suggested by the very prominence of castles in novels frequently termed *Bildungsromane*.

> Diese liebenswürdige Familie lebte in einer Harmonie beisammen, deren Anblick unsern Helden in die selige Einfalt und Unschuld des goldenen Alters versetzte. Niemals hatte er eine so schöne Ordnung, eine so vollkommene Eintracht, ein so regelmäßiges Ganzes gesehen, als das Haus des weisen Archytas darstellte ... Archytas hatte keine Sklaven ... Sie [seine Diener] waren stolz darauf einem so vortrefflichen Herrn zu dienen, ... keine Spur dieses üppigen Übermuts, der gemeiniglich den müßiggängerischen Haufen der Bedienten in großen Häusern bezeichnet ... Das Haus des Archytas glich der innerlichen Ökonomie des animalischen Körpers. [29]

In contrast, the description of the house of Agathon's first mentor, Hippias, serves only to underline the cynical hedonist's amoral relationship to his troubled society. He has spared nothing to make his house „zu einem Tempel der ausgekünsteltesten Sinnlichkeit."[30] „Er wollte, daß die seinigen, in seinem Hause wenigstens, sich nirgends hinwenden sollten, ohne einem gefallenden stand zu begegnen."[31]

Further testing of the suitability of poetic islands for expressing the relationship of the moral hero of the *Bildungsroman* to his society will help answer another of the questions, posed earlier: the one concerning the extent to which the first *Bildungsroman* might be considered a utopian novel. True poetic islands, we remember, are *descriptive*, that is, they serve to portray an individual's real, felt or experienced, relationship to his society. The quasi-island of the first *Bildungsroman*, in contrast, is *prescriptive*, indicating the ideal relationship between the idealistic *Weltverbesserer* and the imperfect, sometimes resentful society he is trying to transform. The question of this relationship is what lies at the heart of the *Bildungsroman*. The somewhat improbable

---

[29]*Agathon*, pp. 458ff.
[30]*Agathon*, p. 58.
[31] *Agathon*, p. 55.

social utopia sketched in the concluding chapters is nothing more than a poetic corroboration of the answer to this question given in the novel. In other words, Wieland is not so much concerned with the description of a utopian society as he is concerned with prescribing the appropriate relationship of the responsible, moral man of vision to the society in which he finds himself.

Before proceeding to a discussion of *Wilhelm Meister* in the next chapter, we may summarize our remarks on the novel to which Goethe's great *Bildungsroman* owes perhaps even more than is generally recognized. In *Agathon* two major European novel traditions converge, the idealistic tradition of the courtly novel and the realistic picaresque tradition. In the eighteenth century the other-worldly idealism of the preceding age had given way to this-worldly morality. Wieland's novel attempts to reconcile the new optimistic utopian hopes for society to the disillusioning experience of the world. Such a reconciliation could not be completely convincing. *Agathon*, like all subsequent *Bildungsromane*, ends with a call to duty and a note of subdued optimism. While the hero is forced to modify his urge to reform and retreat to a tenable position, he is encouraged to keep up the fight against the forces of ignorance and selfishness. The author's parting advice to all would-be Agathons, „daß man in einem großen Wirkungskreise zwar mehr schimmern, aber in einem kleinen mehr Gutes schaffen kann,"[32] will be repeated with slight variations by the inheritors of the tradition well into the twentieth century.

---

[32]*Agathon*, p. 578.

CHAPTER 4: *DIE LEHRJAHRE*

The term *Bildungsroman* is associated more with Goethe's *Wilhelm Meister* than with any other single novel. For many scholars the influence which this work has exerted on subsequent novel production in Germany is equivalent to the history of the *Bildungsroman*. [1] For many, *Wilhelm Meister* represents at once the conception and the culmination of this major novel tradition. As the most important novel of the golden age of German letters, *Wilhelm Meister* has been studied, praised, discussed, damned and misunderstood as much as or more than any other in German literature. Almost from the beginning the catchword *Bildung* has jeopardized the viewing of *Wilhelm Meister* in its proper literary-historical context.

Scholars and casual readers alike have instinctively felt that Goethe provided a key to the understanding of his work and the character of his hero in the famous letter in Book 5 in which Wilhelm informs his friend and brother-in-law Werner of his intention of joining Serlo's troupe.[2] The nascent actor writes:

> Mich selbst, ganz wie ich da bin, auszubilden, das war dunkel von Jugend auf mein Wunsch und meine Absicht.[3]

Because of this avowal, scholars have been concerned with defining and analyzing the *Bildungsgut*, the *Bildungsidee*, the *Bildungsideal*, the *Bildungsziel*, the *Bildungsweg*, the *Bildungsgang*,

---

[1] See Note 17, Chapter 1.

[2] For example, H. A. Korff, *Geist der Goethezeit* (Leipzig: Verlagsbuchhandlung von J. J. Weber, 1930), II, 343. Also Roy Pascal, *The German Novel*, p. 8.

[3] *Wilhelm Meister*, p. 290.

the *Bildungsphasen,* and the *Bildungsstufen* of this classical *Bildungsroman.* Scholarship which proceeds in this direction toward increasingly questionable general abstractions does not reveal the relationship of this novel and its hero to European and German novel traditions. At least for our investigation it seems more fruitful to begin not with the specific questions *what* and *which,* but with the more fundamental *why.* We don't want to ask *what* the nature of Wilhelm's *Bildung* is, nor *what* the phases, steps, and ways that lead to this ideal *Bildung* are, but rather this: *Why is Bildung so important for Wilhelm?*

✳✳✳✳✳✳✳✳✳✳✳✳✳✳

From the discussion of the previous chapter we recall that two considerations were of equal importance to the hero of the first *Bildungsroman.* First, because Agathon is a true lineal descendant of the traditional picaresque hero, he is concerned with the preservation of his own personal integrity. But secondly, because Agathon is also a descendant of the idealistic hero of the courtly novel, preserving his personal integrity involves discharging a moral duty, which, for him, a child of the Enlightenment, is a duty towards society. We saw that Agathon could hope to do justice to both considerations only by reducing his base of operations and retreating strategically to a protected position of relatively limited social contact, activity, and responsibility. Agathon was, first— through study and contemplation within the sanctuary of his castle retreat—to secure his moral personality against the cynicism and treachery of the timeservers and against the dangers resulting from the un-moderated dicta of his ardent, idealistic heart. Secondly, he was to seek—through the example of his personality and way of life—to effect changes for the good in the world about him. If, as we think, *Agathon* represents the prototype of the *Bildungsroman,* the *Bildung* should be important to Wilhelm chiefly to the extent that it helps him meet these two interrelated objectives.

But first we must ask whether Goethe's hero is actually concerned with meeting these twin objectives, which in a short-hand notation we might call *personal survival* and *social reform*. With respect to the first objective, the evidence is obvious and incontrovertible. Wilhelm is concerned about the survival and development of his personality and conscious of the threat to it posed by contemporary social institutions. In the oft-quoted letter to Werner, Wilhelm writes:

> Ein Bürger kann sich Verdienst erwerben und zur höchsten Not seinen Geist ausbilden; seine Personalität geht aber verloren.[4]

Just as the picaresque hero can maintain his personal integrity only as an outsider, so Wilhelm fears that he can maintain his personal integrity, develop his personality, only in the actors' world on the periphery of society. Although many of Wilhelm's ideas at the time of this letter to Werner later proved to be erroneous and delusional, this particular fear, this idea that he must flee the confines of contemporary bourgeois society, is not an illusion, for it is never contradicted by later events and revelations. Goethe very deliberately juxtaposes the two friends at the end of the novel to underline this point. Werner has sacrificed his personality for material success within the confines of bourgeois society. He has been reduced to the passionless, lifeless instrument of his own one-sided ambition. He cuts a pale, sickly figure beside the robust, healthy Wilhelm, who, despite his frequent erring, has been able to develop himself as an individual in his wanderings beyond the frontiers of his bourgeois world.[5]

---

[4]*Wilhelm Meister*, p. 290.
[5]See *Wilhelm Meister*, pp. 498-500.

Wilhelm Meister offers ample specific evidence not only of Wilhelm's concern for his personal survival, but also of Goethe's concern with the problem of the survival of individual personality in modern society. A large body of evidence in Goethe's life and work also suggests that this problem, in varying forms, was a persistent one for Goethe.[6] After the French Revolution, which Goethe viewed from the start as a threat to European culture and intellectual activity,[7] his concern with the problem of the survival of the individual in a fluid society became more intense.

It is not necessary to belabor the point, therefore, that Goethe, as he turned in the 1790's to the task of reworking the *Theatralische Sendung* into the *Lehrjahre*, was eminently concerned with one of the two central problems in *Agathon*: with the picaresque problem of the survival of the individual in his integrity. When we begin to look for evidence that he was equally concerned with the second problem, with the moral imperative of the Enlightenment, with the problem of social reform, the prospect seems at first less promising. If Goethe is against the Revolution, if

---

[6]We note, for example, that Goethe's most memorable characters, from Götz and Werther to Tasso and Faust, are caught up in the conflict between the unconditional demands which their personalities place on the world and the distinctly restricting, confining conditions which both the natural and the civilized world place on their very existence. Compare Wilhelm Mommsen, *Die politischen Anschauungen Goethes* (Stuttgart: Deutsche Verlags-Anstalt, 1948), p. 27: „Was Goethe von Shakespeare sagt, gilt auch vom *Götz*, alles dreht sich um den geheimen Punkt . . ., in dem das eigentümliche unseres Ichs, die präsentierte Freiheit unseres Willens, mit dem notwendigen Gang des Ganzen zusammenstößt."

[7]See Mommsen, p. 109: „Der tiefste Grund für die Ablehnung der Revolution durch Goethe liegt aber darin, daß . . . [sie] . . . die private Existenz des geistigen Menschen in der alten Form unmöglich machte," and p. 113: „Bewußt ist ihm [Goethe] vor allem die unendliche Gefahr, die hier für die Kultur und für die Bildung entsteht."

he mistrusts the ideas put forth by the revolutionists, then he must be a conservative who is concerned more with the retention of the old order than the creation of a new one. In fact, Goethe was concerned with both conservation and change. His opposition to the French Revolution stems from a deep-seated mistrust of revolution in general as a means of social change. By its violence a revolution tends to destroy what was good in the old order along with what was bad. Goethe was for change, but he championed a process of change which would preserve the achievements of the past while remedying its failings. Goethe, throughout his mature life, stood for evolution, not revolution.[8]

When we look in the novel for evidence of Wilhelm's being concerned with the problem of social reform, the first impression is once again misleading. In the letter to Werner from which we have already quoted several times Wilhelm actually states that he is not concerned with influencing society.

> An diesem Unterschied ist . . . die Verfassung der Gesellschaft selbst schuld; ob sich daran einmal etwas ändern wird und was sich ändern wird, *bekümmert mich wenig.*[9] (Emphasis added)

He goes on to say that he is concerned only with his personal survival, with the survival of his personality:

> . . . genug, ich habe, wie die Sachen jetzt stehen, an mich selbst zu denken, und wie ich mich selbst und das, was mir ein unerläßliches Bedürfnis ist, rette und erreiche.[10]

---

[8]Mommsen, p. 32 writes: „. . . daß er Evolution, nicht Revolution wollte, wie das allezeit Goethes Grundauffassungen entsprach."
[9]*Wilhelm Meister*, p. 291.
[10] *Wilhelm Meister*, p. 291.

We need not attach too much weight to this disclaimer. As already suggested, many of the sentiments expressed by Wilhelm in this letter are contradicted by later events and revelations. The mere fact that Wilhelm feels called upon to disavow any altruistic concern with the betterment of society contains at least the germ of the suggestion that the opposite may indeed be true. We must remember that the recipient of this letter, Werner, is a realistic, no-nonsense businessman to whom even Wilhelm's *selfish* ambition—*mich selbst ganz . . . auszubilden*—must seem fantastic. It is the task of the *Bildungsroman*, as we have noted in our investigation of *Agathon*, to remove the fantastic elements from the hero's utopian vision while leaving the essential vision of a better world intact.[11] A direct confrontation here between reality as represented by Werner, and ideal, as striven for by Wilhelm, would result in the discrediting of the ideal. Wilhelm therefore adopts a more realistic, a more selfish stance before Werner than we detect in his actions and behavior with respect to the rest of the world.

There is ample internal evidence to support such an interpretation of Wilhelm's remarks to Werner. His youthful dreams of becoming the creator of a German National Theater prove that the stage meant more to him than just an environment in which he could exercise and develop all aspect of his personality. Wilhelm was animated by a sense of mission, *Sendung*, to fulfill a

---

[11] Compare Schiller's formulation of the goal of *Wilhelm Meister*, to Goethe, July 8, 1796: „Wenn ich das Ziel, bei welchem Wilhelm nach einer langen Reihe von Verirrungen endlich anlagt, mit dürren Worten auszusprechen hätte, so wurde ich sagen: ‚er tritt von einem leeren und unbestimmten Ideal in ein bestimmtes tätiges Leben, aber ohne die idealisierende Kraft dabei einzubüßen.'" Fritz Jonas, ed., *Schillers Briefe* (Stuttgart: Deutsche Verlagsanstalt, 1895), V, p. 22.

national need.[12] His concern with staging a flawless production of *Hamlet* betrays not a desire to win the acclaim of a few connoisseurs and discerning critics in his audience but rather a genuine concern with raising the level of the many.[13] Even in his first early encounter with a troupe of actors there were discussions, we are told, in which the "Einfluss des Theaters auf die *Bildung* einer Nation und der Welt nicht vergessen wurde."[14] For a long time the stage seemed to Wilhelm to be the best means by which he might improve the public. [15] When he learned by bitter experience that the stage is more naturally a reflection of public taste than a molder of public thought, that is, when he learned that the stage was poorly suited to his ultimate aim of molding society, he divorced himself from the theater altogether.

The very letter in which Wilhelm disclaims any concern for social reform contains an implicit contradiction of his disavowal. For although he denies any sense of social responsibility in his quest for "jener harmonischen Ausbildung meiner Natur," [16] Wilhelm admits to Werner that his decision to become an actor stems not only from the actor's usual desire to please, but in his case, also

---

[12]Note that Wilhelm compares himself to the progressive King Henry IV, who, as Prince Hal in Shakespeare's play „sich unter geringer, ja sogar schlechter Gesellschaft eine Zeitlang aufhält." *Wilhelm Meister*, p. 210.

[13]In a discussion with Serlo, for example, Wilhelm argues: „Es ist eine falsche Nachgiebigkeit gegen die Menge, wenn man ihnen die Empfindungen erregt, die sie haben *wollen*, und nicht die, die sie haben *sollen*," (*Wilhelm Meister*, p. 314.) Later Wilhelm's ambition „das Publikum zu bilden" becomes an object of ridicule for Melina. See *Wilhelm Meister*, p 351.

[14]*Wilhelm Meister*, p. 60.

[15]A belief in the poet's or artist's duty to educate and elevate his audience had been made popular in the Enlightenment by the writings of Shaftesbury. See *Characteristics* (Chapter 3, Note 16), pp. 172-73.

[16]*Wilhelm Meister,* p. 291.

from a desire to influence, to effect changes for the good, to *wirken*.[17] *Wirken*, we note, was one of the verbs Wilhelm used to describe the activity of the nobility, in contrast to the *leisten* and *schaffen* of the *Bürger*. The nobleman *wirkt* through his mere being, whereas the burgher can accomplish within the confines of bourgeois society only at the expense of his personal being, his personality. As we shall have cause to note, *wirken* is also the verb used to describe Lothario's socialistic activity later in the novel.[18]

****

On the basis of the above discussion we may conclude that in *Wilhelm Meister* Goethe is indeed concerned with the two basic interrelated objectives central to Wieland's *Agathon*. This hypothesis is further substantiated by convincing internal evidence.

Again we refer to Wilhelm's letter to Werner. The situation of the burgher which Wilhelm describes so poignantly corresponds almost exactly to the situation in which Agathon found himself before his arrival in Tarent. As long as Agathon's efforts at reform were confined to a struggle immediately within the framework and on the terms of contemporary social conditions, he saw his efforts despised, his essential nature unappreciated, and his personality threatened and endangered. Both his deeds and his accomplishments contrasted sharply with those of Archytas, who was able

---

[17]*Wilhelm Meister*, p. 292. Because of the importance of this word in the discussions that follow, and because no exact English translation exists for it, it seems advisable to retain the German here. Similarly the subtlety and many-sidedness of the distinctions between the words *leisten* and *schaffen*, which are used to characterize the activity of the bourgeois, are lost in translation.

[18]*Wilhelm Meister*, p. 431.

to *wirken* merely through his exemplary life and person. Thus, according to the dictum of the first *Bildungsroman*, Wilhelm was correct in assuming that he could effect changes in the world, *wirken*, only by securing his personality, which in turn could be accomplished only through „jene harmonische Ausbildung." This basic assumption is not contradicted by any later insight that Wilhelm eventually acquires, for it is consistent with Goethe's mature Weltanschauung.[19] Restating this important conclusion: Only through "jene harmonische Ausbildung" can Wilhelm hope to secure his personality—in itself a weighty consideration. But the very securing of his personality is in itself as much a means as an end, a prerequisite for the achievement of a second important objective, the betterment of society.[20]

Despite the general concordance between *Wilhelm Meister* and *Agathon* as to the significance of *Bildung* for the main character,

---

[19] The classical poetic formulation of this idea occurs, of course, in *Iphigenie*. The curse of "Tantalus Geschlecht" is a precipitous *Tatendrang* which leads to a vicious circle of horror and destruction. The curse cannot be broken by new deeds. Orestes' heroic sally against King Thoas seems destined only to involve him deeper in guilt and suffering. Iphigenie is able to break the curse by achieving a new level of humanity, the level of the "Schöne Seele," the classically harmonious personality. Because of her elevated position, like the nobility to which Wilhelm refers in his letter, she is able to *wirken*, whereas Orestes, like the Burger in Wilhelm's letter to Werner, had been restricted to the ineffectual *schaffen* and *leisten*.

[20] Approaching the problem from a completely different starting point, Wilhelm Mommsen, p. 264, has arrived at a similar conclusion: "Sein Ideal der harmonischen Persönlichkeit, von dem man so oft gesprochen hat und das man so oft mißverstand, ist doch nicht um seiner selbst willen da. Denn dieses zur menschlichen Höhe ausgebildete Individuum, so sehr es das „Allgemeine" als störend empfindet, hat doch seinen Wert nicht in sich selbst, sondern dadurch, daß es von diesem Wert aus anderen zu geben in der Lage ist."

there are, of course, significant differences. These differences, such as the relatively greater importance of *Bildung* in Goethe's novel, may be to a large extent differences of emphasis rather than of substance—a conclusion which our subsequent analysis will tend to support. One underlying difference between the two novels, however—the fact that Wieland's novel is set remote in time and place, whereas Goethe's is given a domestic setting in the recent past—is substantial.

Without examining the reasons why Wieland chose an antique setting for his novel, we observe that the resulting rather timeless, neutral, "classical" background corresponds to a general way of viewing the problem of the relationship of the individual to his society. For Wieland, the problem could still be cast in very general terms. Agathon's "Geschichte" is the timeless story of the enlightened, moral man in a world characterized by greed and ignorance. Goethe examines this problem from the starting point of a particular manifestation in a specific, defined set of political, social and economic conditions. As we shall see, after explicating the problem in the concrete terms of an individual contemporary experience, he examines both the nature of and solution to the problem in more general, abstract terms.

As we have already noted, Wilhelm Meister is concerned *from the beginning* with the problem of securing his personality. "Das war . . . von Jugend auf mein Wunsch und meine Absicht." [21] He realizes that his personality must be developed, fought for, and won. Agathon is aware of no such problem. His personality is a given entity which remains essentially unchanged throughout the entire story. [22] Agathon learns gradually that he must be on his guard to preserve this given personality against the dissipating

---

[21] See Note 3 above for fuller quotation.

[22] Agathon changes really only in the sense that he becomes *wiser*, that he gains what we earlier called *picaresque* knowledge.

forces of society, but the problem of first developing or obtaining a highly individual personality does not really exist for him. After each crisis which his personality successfully weathers we are merely told that he is "wieder Agathon."[23] This shift in emphasis between *Agathon* and *Wilhelm Meister* from a concern with the problem of retaining a given personality to a concern with the problem of first realizing a personality at all is a measure of the younger poet's greater awareness of the threats to individual integrity posed by the emerging new order.

Wilhelm's concern with acquiring his personality through *Bildung* is presented essentially as a problem peculiar to a particular class of individuals in a definite epoch in European history. The personality of the late-eighteenth-century burgher—according to Goethe's understanding of the situation—is threatened with annihilation from the very moment it begins its embryonic development. In comparison, as Wilhelm notes in the much-cited letter to Werner, the personality of the contemporary nobleman does not seem to be in any danger at all.

The greater emphasis on *Bildung* in *Wilhelm Meister* compared with *Agathon* appears to be a direct result of Goethe's removing the problem from its neutral, classical setting and discussing it in a specific, contemporary framework. Wilhelm, like the typical *Bildungsroman* hero Agathon, is concerned with the twin objectives of personal survival and social reform. However, because he is not just any Agathon, but an eighteenth-century German bourgeois Agathon, he must be concerned relatively more with the first objective. For him, a *Bürger*, the problem of personal survival is immediate and pressing. Though he writes to Werner, "Ich habe . . . viel gewonnen,"[24] it is clear when he meets Lothario in Book 7 that his personality is still a flimsy construction when compared with the

---

[23]See, for example, *Agathon*, pp. 166, 174, 271, 298 and 432.
[24]*Wilhelm Meister*, P. 291.

imperial self-assurance of the nobleman. It is clear that he will have to concern himself more with the securing of his personality through *Bildung* than either Agathon or the contemporary nobleman.

To the extent that we consider their personalities and individual histories, it is, in fact, the nobleman Lothario, rather than the burgher Wilhelm, who represents the most direct literary descendant of Wieland's Agathon.[25] The tendency to equate, at least for purposes of comparison and contrast, the figure of Agathon with that of Wilhelm Meister, has obscured the relationship that exists between the two novels. By positing Lothario as the real Agathon figure in Goethe's novel we discover a new vantage point from which to view the relationship between the two works: Lothario's story, which is recounted synoptically in the last two books, is an explication in general terms of the central *Bildungsroman* problem as it is formulated in Wieland's *Agathon*. Wilhelm's story, the story of an individual in *a specific historico-sociological situation*, is universalized or generalized by the parallel story of Lothario.

From America Lothario had written to Jarno: "Ich werde zurück-kehren und in meinem Hause, in meinem Baumgarten, mitten

---

[25]The parallels between the figure of Agathon and that of Lothario are in fact quite striking. Like Agathon, Lothario grew up fatherless but nevertheless under ideal conditions, in virtual seclusion from the disruptive influences of the outside world. Like Agathon, Lothario has a beautiful sister who represents the human soul (Psyche) in its naïve perfection. Like Agathon, Lothario is presented as being virtually irresistible to most members of the opposite sex. Both Agathon and Lothario did not hesitate to sacrifice to their grander ambitions the women on whom they bestowed their affection. Like Agathon, the main knowledge that Lothario gains from his experience in the world is the need to concern himself more with the preservation of his personal integrity as he goes about the business of social reform.

unter den Meinigen sagen: ‚Hier oder nirgends ist Amerika!'"[26] By that statement Lothario meant merely that instead of exhausting himself fighting for the new order in the world at large across the ocean he would concentrate on establishing it within the manageable confines of his own estate. Whereas the type of agrarian and social reforms he had in mind are only hinted at in the *Lehrjahre*, it is clear that they are uppermost in his mind and that they form the single greatest outlet for his tremendous energies. The main difference between Lothario's efforts at social reform in America and his later efforts on his own estate is the recognition that he must give some thought to the conservation of his own person and personal resources. Like Agathon before him, Lothario has learned by experience of the folly of throwing the whole weight and energy of his personality directly upon the gears and levers of contemporary society. His return from America corresponds to Agathon's farewell to direct political activity in Syracuse and his retreat to Tarent.

When Wilhelm journeys to deliver a letter to Lothario, he is himself just returning from a type of American campaign. His attempt, "in einem weitern Kreise zu wirken"[27] had exposed him to dangers no less real than those Lothario had encountered in America. Gradually Wilhelm learns to draw the parallels between his own experience of the world and Lothario's. In Lothario's retreat to his own estate Wilhelm finds a model for his own behavior. After some slight hesitation he gives up his grandiose plans, bids farewell to the theater, and begins to concern himself with more immediate problems.

From Lothario, Wilhelm learns Agathon's lesson of the necessity of maintaining a balance between contact-with and isolation-from society. If the lordly Lothario must concern himself with personal

---

[26]*Wilhelm Meister*, p. 432. Note the homecoming theme.
[27]*Wilhelm Meister*, p. 292.

survival while going about the ultimate task of social reform, then how much more must he, the poor *Bürgersohn*, be concerned with this problem: Wilhelm's earlier retreat to the stage, from which he had hoped to effect changes in society, may be viewed as a first unsuccessful attempt to achieve this balance. But like Agathon before him, Wilhelm had completely underestimated the magnitude of the threat society represented to his personal integrity. Only when he meets Lothario and becomes acquainted with his modest, but manageable plans for social reform does Wilhelm become aware of the folly of his earlier efforts at changing the world from the stage.[28]

It is significant that Wilhelm, before he actually meets Lothario, pauses to contemplate his castle and its relationship to the surrounding countryside. The description of this castle through Wilhelm's eyes is at once a graphic portrayal of Lothario's dynamic personality and a graphic representation of his relationship to the world about him. The building, which is described as a series of newer structures in various styles extending outward in all directions from an older, irregular, central castle is, in fact, an elaborate symbolic pictograph recording the development of Lothario's personality from the first important impressions imparted by the personality of the *Oheim* and the liberal pedagogy of the Abbé to the subsequent outward testing thrust of his

---

[28] The stage proved to be an unfortunate choice as a base of operations. He had erred in his estimation that the stage was far enough removed from society to insulate him from the dangers it held for his personality. For although the stage was in his day a largely extra-social institution, it was not free of the faults of the society from which it had sprung. The actors' world eventually revealed itself to Wilhelm to be but a microcosmic caricature of the larger realm. As Jarno explained to our disillusioned hero, who had just delivered a resounding condemnation of the theater: "Sie haben nicht das Theater, sondern die Welt beschrieben." *Wilhelm Meister*, p. 434.

personality toward interaction with the world. The haphazard nature of the structure is a reflection of the trial-and-error theory of education to which Lothario had been subjected. [29] It is significant that the guiding architectonic principle—in as much as one is visible—seems to be "innere Bequemlichkeit." This emphasis on comfort, in conjunction with an obvious preference for „nutzbare Gärten" over purely decorative ones, reveals an over-riding concern with utility and practical results. Specific reference to the fact that there is no trace of an encircling wall or moat and the suggested prospect of a cheerful village in the distance serve to remind the reader that while Lothario's castle provides him with secure and comfortable grounds in which he may live and work, it does not isolate him from the world.

It seems to be clear from the above discussions that Lothario is not only a typical Agathon-figure—his castle is also a typical *Bildungsroman* castle which serves him much in the same way that Archytas' villa serves Agathon: It is a fortress against society, but

---

[29]At the end of her *Bekenntnisse* the *Schöne Seele* gives an introduction to this theory (*Wilhelm Meister*, p. 419). Later, as Wilhelm is about to receive his *Lehrbrief*, a figure that could be the Abbé sums up this theory sententiously: „Nicht vor Irrtum zu bewahren, ist die Pflicht des Menschenerziehers, sondern den Irrenden zu leiten, ja ihn seinen Irrtum aus vollen Bechern ausschlurfen zu lassen, das ist Weisheit der Lehrer. Wer seinen Irrtum nur kostet, hält lange damit haus, er freut sich dessen als eines seltenen Glückes, aber wer ihn ganz erschöpft, der muß ihn kennen lernen, wenn er nicht wahnsinnig ist." (*Wilhelm Meister*, p. 495). Natalie criticizes this theory as being „ganz gegen meine Gesinnungen" (p. 527). „Ja, ich mochte behaupten, es sei besser, nach Regeln zu irren, als zu irren, wenn uns die Willkür unserer Natur hin und her treibt, und wie ich die Menschen sehe, scheint mir in ihrer Natur immer eine Lücke zu bleiben, die nur durch ein entschieden ausgesprochenes Gesetz ausgefüllt werden kann." Natalie's castle (the *Oheim's*) is correspondingly regular; it forms a harmonious whole, quite in keeping with her person-ality (p. 527).

also a formative force and a focal point for developments within that society. We note also that in the description of Lothario's castle, as in the description of Archytas' villa, the negative function of the castle—that of protecting the individual—is not emphasized, whereas its positive function receives considerable stress. But Lothario's castle is not Wilhelm's castle. Wilhelm does not stay with Lothario. He visits Lothario's sister, Natalie, whom he eventually marries, and it is in her quite different castle, the one she inherits from the *Oheim*, that Wilhelm experiences a homecoming comparable to Agathon's arrival in Tarent. Before examining this most important of the castles in *Wilhelm Meister*, however, we must look more closely at Goethe's understanding of the specifically contemporary aspects of the general *Bildungsroman* problem.

****

As we recall from the discussion in Chapters 1 and 2, the *Bildungsroman*, in general, may be considered a product of a new social mobility occasioned by the emergence of new forces and concepts and the consequent breakdown of the old order. In eighteenth-century Europe the rapid increase in the importance of trade relative to that of land as a source of wealth was the strongest force working for the overthrow of the old order. Goethe was especially disturbed by the shift of power from the landed nobility to the bourgeois merchant because of his conception of the role and function of the various social classes. According to him, every individual is born with certain natural talents and inclinations. It is the duty of each individual to discover and develop his talents to the best of his ability. By doing so he becomes a productive member of society. Similarly, for Goethe, each social class has its special area of competency and, correspondingly, specific duties with respect to the whole of society.[30] Goethe feared general chaos and cultural regression as a result of the blurring of class distinctions.

The roles that Goethe envisaged for the nobility and the bourgeoisie corresponded by and large to the roles they had played in European society for several centuries.[31] The nobility was to be the ruling class, whereas the bourgeoisie was to cultivate the arts, the sciences, and the crafts.[32] The acquisition of great wealth by the bourgeoisie was regarded by Goethe as a danger for Europe for several reasons. In the first place, a bourgeois concerned with the acquisition of great wealth tended to neglect his bourgeois duties, with the resulting decline of the arts, sciences, and crafts. But secondly, great wealth in the hands of the bourgeoisie tended to undermine the economic base for the political power of the

---

[30]Compare Mommsen, p. 114: „Freiheit bedeutet für Goethe, daß der einzelne seine Persönlichkeit gemäß seinem Wesen ausbilden und eine diesem Wesen und seinem Stande gemäße Tätigkeit ausüben kann."

[31]With the important difference that Goethe played down the earlier economic role of the bourgeoisie. See next note.

[32]See Mommsen, p. 249: "Goethe hielt, wie wir sahen, Zeit seines Lebens an der Auffassung fest, daß das Regieren die Sache der dazu Berufenen und durch Geburt bestimmten Schichten sei." Also, p. 252: „Das Verhältnis Bürgertum-Adel verliert für Goethe schon dadurch den Charakter eines Konfliktes, weil ja von seiner Auffassung aus beide Stände nebeneinander ihre eigene Aufgabe haben. Das Bürgertum umfaßt dabei Bildung und Besitz, sowie das Handwerk." And. p. 267: „Die bürgerlichen Schichten sind für Goethe, was ja auch weitgehend zutraf, die Träger von Kunst und Wissenschaft. Hier findet der Burger die ihm gemäße Aufgabe, während die wirtschaftliche Funktion des Bürgertums für Goethe sehr stark zurücktritt."

nobility, with resulting socio-political chaos.[33] And again, without the political stability guaranteed by the traditional ruling class, Goethe thought little could be accomplished in the field of the arts, sciences, and crafts.

Thus, Goethe saw two specific problems facing his contemporaries. The bourgeoisie must be saved from its self-destructive concern with money and re-confirmed in its role as bearer of European culture. Secondly, the nobility must be re-established on a firm economic basis so that it might continue to play its traditional role of political leadership.

****

The extent to which Goethe is concerned in *Wilhelm Meister* with the unpropitious drift of contemporary society is not indicated by the plot of the novel. This concern, however, which forms the necessary reference point for a proper understanding of *Wilhelm Meister*, is clearly indicated by the consistency with which Goethe represents the cultural decline of the bourgeoisie over three generations. Goethe achieves this representation with the utmost in economy and precision by working in the seemingly unrelated and incidental description of three separate *Bürgerhäuser* from three successive generations.

The *Bürgerhaus*, of course, should be the burgher's castle. It should protect him from the vagaries of social life without isolating him from society. The first indication that something is wrong in Wilhelm's bourgeois castle is given by his discontent with the life in his father's house. Wilhelm's paternal home, which represents the

---

[33]Mommsen, p. 268: „Er [Goethe] rechnet jedenfalls das emporsteigende reiche Bürgertum nicht zu dem, was er selbst unter Bürgertum versteht. Er empfindet, wie sehr diese Schicht die alte ständische Gliederung die ihr zugrundeliegende Lebensführung sprengen mußte, . . .“

middle generation of the three presented in the novel, is richly furnished "nach dem neuesten Geschmack," [34] but it seems "empty"[35] to him. The home of the preceding generation, in contrast, which housed his grandfather's magnificent art collection, was a wonderful, exciting treasure trove for the young hero, "full," in other words, of many things to occupy and satisfy a healthy, young curiosity. Finally, the house which represents the third generation is "empty" not only in the mind of the child, but in fact. Werner writes to Wilhelm that in this little "nest" he has room enough only for his desk.[36]

The cultural decline of the bourgeoisie within three generations parallels the growing bourgeois obsession with money-making. It was Wilhelm's father's concern with money-making that blinded him to the cultural value of the family art collection. Since he could see in this collection only its potential monetary value, he sold it upon the death of the grandfather. Although he earmarked most of the money realized by the sale for re-investment, Wilhelm's father still retained a substantial portion of the money in order to refurbish and refurnish his house. When he in turn left his worldly possessions to the care of the following generation, they too were promptly converted into money for investment. But such was the young Werner's concern with making money that he could not even appreciate the traditional bourgeois comforts of a fine house and rich furnishings.

The older Meister's decision to sell the art collection and then to redecorate his home "nach dem neuesten Geschmack" is a measure of the extent to which the bourgeoisie, in its quest for

---

[34] *Wilhelm Meister*, p. 40.
[35] *Wilhelm Meister*, p. 12.
[36] *Wilhelm Meister*, pp.286-87. In describing his new accommodations Werner specifically calls attention to those of the previous two generations.

ever greater wealth, has relinquished its role as custodian and transmitter of traditional cultural values. Once the self-confident, knowledgeable, independent patron and originator of the arts and sciences, the emerging new bourgeois merchant, divorced and estranged from his natural heritage, has become wholly dependent upon the arbitrary dictates of contemporary fashion for his concepts of worth and permanence. The suggestion is implicitly clear that had conditions not deteriorated to this point, Wilhelm would have been able to complete his *Lehrjahre* at home, that is, in a bourgeois castle. Wilhelm's false start as an actor is intimately related to the failure of his bourgeois environment to provide the necessary conditions for him to become a whole personality, for his *Bildung*.[37] In the barren, *empty* environment of his father's house, the little puppet theater—the one object that seemed to offer contact with other times and other worlds—became Wilhelm's principal interest and, temporarily, the most important factor in his formation.

****

When the art collection was sold by Wilhelm's father it was not dispersed, as well might have happened, but was purchased in its

---

[37]Significantly, after composing a letter to Mariane outlining his plan to flee his bourgeois world and become an actor, Wilhelm meets the Abbé (as the *Unbekannter*), who asks him: "Sind Sie nicht ein Enkel des alten Meisters, der die schöne Kunstsammlung besaß?" (*Wilhelm Meister*, p. 68). When the Abbé suggests then that, had the art collection not been sold, Wilhelm would have a different perspective on the world and himself, the poor *Bürgersohn* is deaf to the significance of his words. Wilhelm's reply, which serves to introduce the Abbé's famous speech on *Schicksal*, merely underlines the connection between the loss of the collection and the false career as an actor *(Wilhelm Meister, pp. 70-71).*

entirety by the *Oheim*. The *Oheim's* castle, which houses and preserves this collection, may be regarded as a symbol for the important element that had passed out of bourgeois society. The *Oheim* was, like Wilhelm's grandfather, a member of the upper bourgeoisie, but he had no bourgeois heirs to whom he could entrust the bourgeois cultural heritage. At one point the *Oheim* specifically mentioned his decision to leave his castle only to someone who could appreciate its value and exemplary significance.[38] When he leaves his castle and its priceless contents to Natalie, responsibility for the European cultural heritage appears to pass symbolically from bourgeoisie to nobility.

The nobility represented by Natalie and members of the *Turmgesellschaft* is, of course, anything but a true likeness of the hereditary nobility of late eighteenth-century Germany. It is a nobility of spirit and duty rather than one of birth and privilege. The tremendous gulf that seemed to Wilhelm to separate the bourgeois from the nobleman in the famous first letter to Werner has narrowed considerably by the end of Book 7.[39] Goethe seems to be exploring a new option to a rigid class structure in the creation of the *Turmgesellschaft*, a new option, but one not radically different from an idealized conception of the old order. Within the *Turmgesellschaft* the ideas, ideals, and relationships of the old order remain—with the important distinction that here privileges and duties are more a function of individual merit and ability than of birth.

---

[38] *Wilhelm Meister*, p. 410: The *Schöne Seele* reports of the *Oheim*: „Wegen des kleinen Gutes, auf dem wir uns befanden, schien er besondere Gedanken zu hegen: ‚Ich werde es," sage er, ‚nur einer Person überlassen, die zu kennen, zu schätzen und zu genießen weiß, was es enthält, und die einsieht, wie sehr ein Reicher und Vornehmer besonders in Deutschland Ursache habe, etwas Mustermäßiges aufzustellen.'"

[39] See Erich Trunz' note to p. 461 of *Wilhelm Meister*.

The new order evolving in the *Turmgesellschaft* bears a close resemblance to the old order largely because Goethe felt that the old order, with its clear division of classes, was in fact a natural order, an order in which—at least in its conception or idealized form—duties and privileges accord to a high degree with individual abilities and merit. Goethe apparently believes that this natural order will establish itself whenever conditions prevail which allow the individual to discover at an early age his own talents and inclinations. A strong, persistent, force operating unilaterally on an individual is contrary to the freedom necessary for natural development. In late eighteenth-century Germany the growing bourgeois obsession with money was such a force. Goethe apparently considered the nobility still relatively free of this and other obsessions. For that reason he had the *Oheim* seek an alliance with the nobility. It was possible, it seemed, to create within this segment of the existing social structure a community in which the natural order would be free to develop. Within such a community the *Oheim* would be able to find a suitable heir and custodian of the cultural heritage represented by the art collection.

The art collection and the Oheim's castle which houses it are of course more than just a symbol of the cultural heritage which had been renounced by the new bourgeoisie. They are an expression of this culture, and, as such, a real force that may act upon the developing human personality in a formative way. The power of such "lifeless" objects [40] to influence the development of the individual was first suggested, as we noted, in Wilhelm's early conversation with the Abbé, who mused on the effect that the sale of the art collection may have had on the young man. This theme is developed more explicitly in Book 6, where the *Schöne Seele*

---

[40] *Wilhelm Meister*, p. 71. Wilhelm refers to the objects in his grandfather's art collection as "leblose Bilder."

describes the *Oheim's* castle and records the deep impression that the acquaintance with it made on her.[41]

It is soon made clear that the effect that the castle has on the *Schöne Seele* is anything but accidental. The *Oheim* has assembled and organized his collection with the express intention of preserving and imparting the necessary prerequisites for any true comprehension of the value and dignity of a work of art, of cultural, artistic tradition.[42] Where such appreciation is lacking, a threat to the very survival of art is present. A collection such as the one Wilhelm's grandfather had assembled, or the larger one, the *Oheim's*, into which it was assimilated, represents, thus, more than just the physical preservation of a cultural tradition in the form of the artistic manifestations of that tradition. More significantly, such a collection represents the only means by which contact with that tradition may be maintained, contact which, in turn, sustains the inner life and growth of the individual and is necessary for the continuing growth of the culture.

As the sale of the art collection by Wilhelm's father indicates, the magnificence of a collection gives no assurance that it will escape destruction in a world where the most powerful forces play without reference to concepts such as cultural tradition and artistic value. And as Wilhelm's mistaken denunciation of the collection as "leblose Bilder" (See note 40) demonstrates, the effect which such

---

[41]*Wilhelm Meister*, p. 401: „Zum erstenmal in meinen Leben erregte mir der Eintritt in ein Haus Bewunderung"; p. 402: „Wie verwundert war ich . . . über den ernsten und harmonischen Eindruck, den ich beim Eintritt in das Haus empfand, und der sich in jedem Saal und Zimmer verstärkte. Hatte Pracht und Zierrat mich sonst nur zerstreut, so fühlte ich mich hier gesammelt und auf mich zurückgeführt"; p. 404: „Nun war ich zum erstenmal durch etwas Äußerliches auf mich selbst zurückgeführt."

[42]Thus the *Oheim* seeks to convince the Schöne Seele „daß eigentlich die Geschichte der Kunst allein uns den Begriff von dem Wert und der Würde eines Kunstwerkes geben könne." *Wilhelm Meister*, p. 408.

a collection can have on an impressionable individual is fully realized only through long exposure. Goethe reaffirms this conviction by describing the *Schöne Seele's* later relationship to the *Oheim's* castle and collection. While her initial impression was characterized by awe at the beauty and harmony of the entirety, wonder at its power to induce in her a feeling of inner concentration, her appreciation and understanding of it were actually very limited. Under the guidance and tutelage of the *Oheim* her eyes were opening to the true worth of the castle and its furnishings. But upon leaving the sphere dominated by the *Oheim* she quickly returned to her former, simpler persuasions.[43]

The role that the *Schöne Seele* plays in Goethe's novel, though central, is obviously ambivalent. On the one hand, she is an exemplary character whose memoirs the members of the *Turmgesellschaft* deem suitable reading for the erring Wilhelm. But on the other hand, she is regarded by the *Oheim* as someone whose influence might endanger the developing personalities of the children Lothario, Natalie, Friedrich, and their sister, *die schöne Gräfin*.[44] The apparently paradoxical relationship of the members of the *Turmgesellschaft* to Natalie's aunt is best explained if we

---

[43]The *Schöne Seele* later confesses, "Ich war gewohnt, ein Gemälde und einen Kupferstich nur anzusehen wie die Buchstaben eines Buches. Ein schöner Druck gefällt mir wohl; aber wer wird ein Buch des Druckes wegen in die Hand nehmen? So sollte mir auch eine bildliche Darstellung etwas sagen, sie sollte mich belehren, rühren, bessern; und der Oheim mochte in seinen Briefen, mit denen er seine Kunstwerke erläuterte, reden, was er wollte, so blieb es mir doch immer beim alten."

[44] The *Schöne Seele* herself calls our attention to this: „Aber, daß, was ich nicht an diesem Erziehen billigen kann, ist, daß sie alles von den Kindern zu entfernen suchen, was sie zu dem Umgange mit sich selbst und mit dem unsichtbaren, einzigen treuen Freunde fuhren könne. Ja, es verdrieß mich oft von dem Oheim, daß er mich deshalb für die Kinder für gefährlich hält." *Wilhelm Meister*, p. 419.

regard her story on the one hand as a warning for Wilhelm and the other as a foil to the other *Schöne Seele* in the novel, to Natalie herself.[45]

That the *Schöne Seele's* memoirs may indeed be regarded as a warning to Wilhelm is indicated by the fact they are worked into the novel in Book 6, just at the point when Wilhelm begins— unwittingly, to be sure—to react to the more direct warning of Book 5, "Flieh, Jüngling, flieh!" These memoirs record the story of a young personality warped by conditions that recall the cultural privations of Wilhelm's youth. During her childhood illness, when she was particularly receptive or impressionable, the *Schöne Seele* had pieced together a picture of the world out of the pitiful little fragments carried to her bedside: a biblical story, a fairy tale, a slain wild hare. Like Wilhelm, who in the "empty" house of his father had seized upon the little puppet theater as a door to a fuller, larger world, the *Schöne Seele* had been forced constantly to call upon her own resources, initiative, and imagination to complete her picture of the world. The result was a spiritually and emotionally ingrown partial recluse who was peculiarly incapable of playing an active role in society. Her situation corresponds to the extreme of "isolation from" society, the polar position to that in which Wilhelm finds himself at the end of Book 5, a position which, as we noted already in Chapter 2, is characterized by too much "contact with" the dissipating forces in his society. The warning implicit in Book 6

---

[45] We may think of the relationship between aunt and niece in the following terms. We marvel at the personality of the *Schöne Seele* much in the same way that we marvel at a flower that has sprung up through a crack in the pavement. We are not impressed by the wholeness, the soundness, or the beauty of the flower but by the fact that there is a flower there at all. The *Schöne Seele* of Book 6 is a flower that has grown to maturity under forbidding circumstances. Her niece, as becomes clear in the discussions which follow, is a similar flower that has been cultivated under the most carefully controlled, ideal conditions.

for Wilhelm is that, in his necessary flight from too much contact with society, he should be careful to avoid the opposite extreme of too little.

The *Schöne Seele* is a perfect foil to her beautiful, well-balanced niece both in terms of their contrasting childhood experiences and their contrasting adult personalities. Because Natalie enjoyed advantages as a child undreamed of by the young *Schöne Seele*, she has been able to develop her personality without sacrificing her position as an active member of society. The advantages that Natalie enjoyed over her aunt are, of course, those provided by the *Oheim* in his castle. Whereas the aunt had to rely on her own imagination to complete her understanding of the world, Natalie grew up in a world literally fraught with interpretive pictures.

One of the chief functions of the *Schöne Seele*'s memoirs, it would seem, is to underline the importance of a castle such as the *Oheim*'s in the education or *Bildung* of the contemporary burgher. Wilhelm, who had lived for a few critical years in such a castle, the *Bürgerhaus* of his grandfather, enjoyed a certain advantage over the *Schöne Seele*, and was consequently in the end not forced to pay the same heavy price. And Natalie, who enjoyed the full benefit of such a castle, was not aware at all of a struggle to achieve her personality.[46]

---

[46]It might be objected that the differences between Natalie and her can be explained by the fact that the *Schöne Seele* is a *Bürgerin* and Natalie, through her father, a member of the nobility. Such a consideration completely ignores the fact that the chief influence operating on the children of the *Schöne Seele*'s sister comes from the *Oheim*, who is a member of the bourgeoisie, a representative of it in its former, more "natural" form, when it was the guardian and transmitter of traditional cultural values.

Not knowing this struggle, Natalie could direct her energies toward others.[47] The *Schöne Seele*, who admires her niece's ability to concern herself with the needs of others, fails to realize that her own inability to be so concerned is a direct result of the deprivation of her childhood.[48] For her, the cultivation of her inner self has become an end in itself. She freely criticizes the *Oheim* and the Abbé for not allowing their charges to be more concerned with their own person.[49] Her point of view, however, is, as we have seen, contrary to the moral thrust of the *Bildungsroman*, and is not long left unchallenged. So that Wilhelm will not be confused on this point, Natalie alludes to the tragedy that is the life of her remarkable aunt: "Eine schwache Gesundheit, *vielleicht zu viel Beschäftigung mit sich selbst* . . . ließ sie das der Welt nicht sein, was sie unter andern Umständen hätte sein können,"[50] (emphasis added).

The conclusion that Natalie's secure personality and her consequent ability to concern herself with the welfare of others is a direct result of her fortunate life in her *Oheim*'s castle is supported by the fact that at several points the physical

---

[47] Natalie did not even have to be on her guard, as did her brother Lothario, against the possibility of losing her personal integrity in a direct confrontation with the world, since there was—due, perhaps to Goethe's conception of the role of women in society—never any suggestion that she would leave her castle retreat. Her concern with the welfare of others is such a significant aspect of her personality that it becomes the object her brother Friedrich's ready wit. (See, for example, *Wilhelm Meister*, p. 565.)

[48] Such is her estrangement from society that she even admits to a certain awkwardness and disinclination in performing the traditional Christian charitable act of almsgiving. But of Natalie she writes, "Gerade das Gegenteil lobte ich an meiner Nichte," (*Wilhelm Meister*, p. 418).

[49] See note 44, above.

[50] *Wilhelm Meister*, p. 517.

resemblance between Natalie and the *Schöne Seele* is stated expressly[51]—for the eighteenth-century reader a clear sign of a fundamental similarity of spirit or soul. In other words, the differences between the personalities of the aunt and her niece must be thought of as resulting from environment or as being manifestations of differences in upbringing and childhood experiences. Since the educational theories to which the *Oheim* subscribes permit no coercion or even direction on the part of the guardian or educator, [52] the influence of the *Oheim*'s castle, with its art collection, on the developing personality of Wilhelm's future bride is emphasized the more.

If Natalie's experience of her *Oheim*'s castle and art collection had done no more than instill in her an active concern for the problems and needs of her fellow men, she would not have become the exemplary *Schöne Seele* that she obviously is in Books 7 and 8 of the *Lehrjahre*. Natalie's long association with the carefully selected monuments of European art freed her from undue concern with herself and nourished the full development of her personality to the point that she herself, her very person, became a sort of living work of art. Like a true work of art—and much like Archytas in *Agathon*—Natalie is able to effect changes in the world about her (*wirken*) by virtue of her mere being.[53]

---

[51]In Book 6, for example (p. 417) the *Schöne Seele* writes of Natalie, "daß sie mir ähnlich sah." In Book 8, p. 517, Wilhelm mistakes a picture of the aunt for the niece.

[52]See note 29 above.

[53]Whenever Goethe mentions Natalie's role as an *Erzieherin* the stress is laid on the influence of her presence, not on any specific knowledge or habits she has to impart. Thus: „Ihre *Gegenwart* hatte den reinsten Einfluß auf junge Mädchen und Frauenzimmer von verschiedenem Alter . . . „ (p. 526; my emphasis). And as Natalie herself says: „Sie wissen vielleicht, daß ich immer eine Anzahl junger Mädchen um mich habe, deren Gesinnungen Ich, indem sie *neben mir* aufwachen, zum Guten und

Thus the *Oheim*'s castle resembles the typical *Bildungsroman* castle, as abstracted from *Agathon*, to the extent that it helps the individual to survive and mature as a whole person and one therefore interested in and capable of exerting a positive influence on the community around him. But in contradistinction to the typical *Bildungsroman* castle, the emphasis here is on the function of protection and defense, not on that of guidance and leadership for the community. There is no evidence of any direct influence of this castle upon the surrounding community such as was patent in Archytas' Tarent. Only individuals, like the young girls in Natalie's care, who spend considerable time within the castle itself are molded by its influence and, presumably, will eventually spread its influence indirectly through the community. And the very building itself, a sort of cultural vault in which an artistic heritage is saved from threatened destruction in the bourgeois world that had earlier produced it, stresses the defensive character. This castle is a metamorphosis of the typical *Bildungsroman* castle resulting from Goethe's decision to state the general *Bildungsroman* problem in contemporary terms. Symbolically it meets or corrects the contemporary evil or danger which Goethe saw as the fundamental one, namely the sacrifice by part of the bourgeoisie of their cultural heritage, their natural cultural and social functions and responsibilities, and first and foremost of their very personalities, because of their obsession with increasing their wealth and power. But Goethe also saw the concomitant

---

Rechten zu bilden wünsche," (p. 514; my emphasis). Jarno's remark, "Therese dressiert ihre Zöglinge, Natalie bildet sie," (p. 532) suggests the special nature of Natalie's influence. Wilhelm expects to benefit from much the same type of influence when he writes to Werner: „Ich verlasse das Theater und verbinde mich mit Männern, deren *Umgang* mich in jedem Sinne zu einer reinen und sichern Tätigkeit fuhren muß" (p. 491; my emphasis).

development, likewise as an evil or danger, namely that the growing financial power of the bourgeoisie must undermine the economic basis of the nobility's political power. Though Lothario is presented in fairly general terms as a typical *Bildungsroman* hero with a typical life story and a typical castle, all after the fashion of Agathon, Lothario is also a representative of the nobility and so is exposed to the contemporary threat to his ability to act effectively for the well-being of society. To meet this evil or danger Goethe has created a second, atypical castle, Therese's modest country estate.

The casual reader remembers Therese as the second girl Wilhelm *almost* marries. His decision to propose to Therese, like his desire to marry Mariane, was a patent mistake. Therese could not offer Wilhelm what he needed most—what was lacking in his own personality—for, in a number of respects, the two were too much alike. [54] What is explicit and dominant in her personality—her exemplary bourgeois virtues of industry, thrift, and loyalty—are never far below the surface of Wilhelm's romantic, idealistic, sometimes Bohemian exterior. [55] Therese's personality, on the other hand, offers the perfect complement to that of Lothario,

---

[54] What is lacking in Wilhelm's personality, we remember, is symbolized by what was lacking, after the sale of the art collection, in his parental home. A similar lack exists in Therese's modest *Landhaus*. Goethe calls our attention to this void, but without specifically making the connection with Wilhelm's home and without observing the contrast with Natalie's castle, which Wilhelm has not yet seen: „Sie ließ Wilhelm allein, und er brachte seinen Abend mit Revision der kleinen Bibliothek zu; sie war wirklich bloß durch Zufall zusammengekommen." *Wilhelm Meister*, p. 460.

[55] We note, for example, how easy it was for Wilhelm to assume the traditional bourgeois virtues in Book 8, „In diesem Sinne waren seine Lehrjahre geendigt, und mit dem Gefühl des Vaters hatte er auch alle Tugenden eines Bürgers erworben." *Wilhelm Meister*, p. 502.

Wilhelm's alter ego among the nobility.[56] Her thrift and orderliness provide the necessary counterbalance to his aristocratic extravagance. Lothario's debt-ridden estate, in turn, provides Therese with a natural object for her managerial talents and energies.[57]

The complementary aspects of Lothario's and Therese's personalities are, as we would expect, reflected and symbolized in their respective castles. Lothario's castle, we remember, reflects in its rambling architecture the young nobleman's constant, somewhat reckless striving toward interaction with the world. Therese's *Landhaus*, on the other hand, is an expression of her personal entelechy as home economist. No aspect of her little estate is described which is not, to a greater or lesser extent, a reflection of her concern with the ultimate in thrift, order and husbandry.[58]

---

[56] Lothario specifically mentions the complementary nature of their personalities as one of the most important elements in their relationship. *Wilhelm Meister*, p. 467.

[57] It is toward such a harmonious union, we remember, that the conciliatory, non-tragic movement of the *Bildungsroman* tends. If instead of Lothario, Wilhelm had married Therese, the stage would have been set for tragedy in the manner of the *Wahlverwandtschaften*, with Wilhelm soon discovering his true passion for Natalie, and Therese consuming herself in her noble renunciation of Lothario. Such a conflict, however, with its necessarily tragic resolution, is foreign to the conception of the *Bildungsroman*.

[58] As an example we may cite a description of her estate as it appeared to Wilhelm: „Sie ließ ihn, als sie zu Hause anlangten, in ihrem kleinen Garten, in welchem er sich kaum herumdrehen konnte; so eng waren die Wege, und so reichlich war alles bepflanzt. Er mußte lächeln, als er über den Hof zurückkehrte, denn da lag das Brennholz so akkurat gesägt, gestalten und geschränkt, als wenn es ein Teil des Gebaudes wäre und immer so liegenbleiben sollte. Rein standen alle Gefäße an ihren Plätzen,

Therese's devotion and her managerial talents assure her husband-to-be of a firm financial basis for the accomplishment of his social reforms. It is significant that Goethe did not seek a more direct solution to Lothario's financial troubles. A wife from Wilhelm's social class, for example, say a sister to Wilhelm or Werner, might well have brought Lothario not only Therese's bourgeois virtues, but a fortune as well.[59] The bourgeoisie, after all, appears in the novel as the inheritor of economic power. It would be only natural for the financially faltering nobility to seek strength and revitalization from this source.[60] But Goethe was apparently unable to reconcile Therese's idealized character traits with his vision of the emerging bourgeois society. As we have noted, there is, according to Goethe, something unwholesome and unholy about the new bourgeoisie which precludes its playing an exemplary role. In seeking to revitalize—symbolically—the nobility, Goethe therefore deliberately bypasses upper bourgeois stock. In fact, the bride Goethe selects for the nobleman, Therese, does not belong exclusively to any class. It is perhaps of some symbolical significance that the barrier to her marriage with Lothario is removed only when the fact is established.

The joint enterprise undertaken by Werner and Lothario at the end of the novel seems to militate against our assumption of an essential incompatibility between the members of the *Turmgesellschaft* and the nouveaux riches. In fact, however, the

---

das Häuschen war weiß und rot angestrichen und lustig anzusehen." *Wilhelm Meister*, p. 445.

[59]Lothario even mentions that his *Oheim* had wanted him to marry a wealthy girl, „er wolle ihm eine reiche Frau geben." *Wilhelm Meister*, p. 456.

[60]Of course, marriages between land-poor nobility and wealthy bourgeois, a phenomenon which became quite common in the nineteenth century, was already a fact of life in the eighteenth.

differences between Werner and Wilhelm's new friends, who regard his brother-in-law with a mixture of pity and scorn, are more visible than ever by the beginning of the last book. Lothario's collaboration with Werner, rather than signaling a basic rapprochement between the two groups, is merely a sign of the new financial muscle of the enlightened landed class, which once again is equal to the economic challenge of the bourgeoisie.

It need not concern us that the supposed new economic independence of the nobility was largely a figment of Goethe's imagination, or that Lothario's social reforms could probably not be financed by the managerial reforms introduced by Therese.[61] What is of interest to us is the general direction of Goethe's thinking, which is essentially conservative. His veneration of the past—conveyed so graphically by the *Saal der Vergangenheit* in the *Oheim*'s castle—is an expression of a deep-seated mistrust of the present. The choice of Therese for Lothario reaffirms this mistrust. Therese's *Landhaus*, much like Natalie's castle, is primarily a fortress against the present, a sanctuary in which the values and

---

[61] To be sure, the nobleman's estate will be more productive and financially independent under Therese's management, but there is an upper boundary in productivity which is determined by things beyond Therese's control, such as the amount and quality of the landed resources at her disposal. Given the technology of the late eighteenth century, even the most effective land management could not provide an economic counter to the growing importance of trade and capital as a source of wealth. Agronomy or husbandry is concerned with maximizing the productivity of a given quantity of resources. Trade and money management, as it came to be practiced in the eighteenth and subsequent centuries, is concerned with increasing the productive base, with the acquisition of new capital and new capital assets. The upper limit to the wealth that may be acquired by this type of activity, for all practical purposes, does not exist, or, if it does exist, is a function of an individual's entrepreneurial skill.

ideals of the past are vindicated and preserved, it is hoped, for the future. Land was the traditional source of income and wealth for the nobility, and Goethe seems to regard it as the only natural source of wealth. Therese's keen business sense, her close attention to detail, and her overriding concern with economy are applauded without reservation. A basically similar attitude and concern on the part of Werner is by implication rejected as un-natural.[62] In Therese's loving but expert management of the land Goethe hopes to establish an effective counter to Werner's unnatural but effective preoccupation with money. Her *Landhaus* becomes a model of agronomical and domestic perfection which seems to offer economic independence to the nobility without compromising their personalities in a direct confrontation with the new forces in bourgeois society. Thus even Therese's manor, though a relatively minor castle designed to answer a specific, contemporary aspect of the general *Bildungsroman* problem, is a *Bildungsroman* castle, however atypical, for it helps Lothario achieve the twin objectives of the *Bildungsroman* hero: the objectives of personal survival and social reform.

---

[62] The fact that Werner's concern with the management of his money inhibits his personal development most decidedly, whereas Therese's concern with the management of her estate does not interfere with the development of a harmonious, health personality, is the best illustration.

CHAPTER 5: STIFTER AND KELLER: A TRADITION IN TRANSITION

Stifter's *Der Nachsommer*

Although sixty years separate the appearance of *Nachsommer* in the mid-nineteenth century and the publication of Goethe's epochal *Wilhelm Meister* in 1797, the Austrian Stifter's experiences of his time was akin to Goethe's experience of his own age, and the two novels, though separated further by a considerable difference in artistic scope and power, touch each other at all major points of theme, problems, and extra-artistic intentions. The questions, problems, and views that are developed and discussed in *Nachsommer* are essentially those that lie at the heart of the earlier novel, and, as shall become clear in the course of this chapter, the ways in which Stifter's novel differs from *Wilhelm Meister* correspond, in a large measure, to the Austrian poet's desire to recreate the Goethean novel for his time.

In the years immediately following the publication of the *Lehrjahre* the most significant novel production in Germany represented a decided reaction to and rejection of the tenets and assumptions of Goethe's great *Bildungsroman*. The central question posed by the *Bildungsroman*, the question as to the relationship of the moral hero to a society in a state of flux, did not seem to the romanticist to be an adequate subject of his *Universalpoesie*.[1] A generation later, when the romantic reaction

---

[1] On the whole, the romantic literature is not concerned with man in a social context so much as with man in a cosmic context, not so much with man in his relationship to historical institutions as with man in his

had largely run its course, the question of the relationship of the individual to contemporary society once again became topical, but the answers provided by the *Bildungsroman* no longer seemed adequate. Immermann's *Die Epigonen* captures the mood of a tormented generation, oppressed by a great tradition which it cannot hold and a future which it cannot accept. Like Goethe's Wilhelm, Immermann's Hermann retreats in the end to a castle which, like the *Oheim*'s in *Wilhelm Meister*, is a sort of cultural vault in an expanding cultural wasteland. But in Immermann's novel there is no suggestion, as there was in Goethe's, that this castle may also have a positive function with respect to the troubled society. For Hermann, the castle becomes an island, one on which it is possible to escape from the present into the past, but an island, nevertheless, and one that is destined to disappear beneath the rising tide of industrialism.[2]

The first volume of Heinrich Laube's *Das Junge Europa* (which appeared several years before *Die Epigonen*) brings disillusionment

---

relationship to eternal verities. It is not accidental that a romantic movement in literature generally follows a period of optimistic revolutionary activity, and that it coincides with or slightly precedes a period of general disillusionment with revolutionary ideals.

[2] See *Die Epigonen*, in *Immermanns Werke*, ed. Harry Mayne (Leipzig and Vienna: Bibliographisches Institut, n.d.), IV, 265-66: "Vor allen Dingen sollen die Fabriken eingehen und die Ländereien dem Ackerbau zurückgegeben werden. Jene Anstalten, künstliche Bedürfnisse künstlich zu befriedigen, erscheinen mir geradezu verderblich und schlecht. Die Erde gehört dem Pfluge, dem Sonnenscheine und Regen, welcher das Samenkorn entfaltet, der fl
eißigen, einfach arbeitenden Hand. Mit Sturmesschnelligkeit eilt die Gegenwart einem trocknen Mechanismus zu; wir können ihren Lauf nicht hemmen, sind aber nicht zu schelten, wenn wir für uns und die Unsrigen ein grünes Plätzchen abzäunen und diese Insel so lange als möglich gegen den Sturz der vorbeirauschenden industriellen Wogen befestigen."

and resignation. Gutzkow's *Ritter vom Geist* represents the first attempt in nineteenth-century Germany to answer positively within a novel the question that lies at the heart of the *Bildungsroman*.[3] Misunderstanding the central thrust of Goethe's novel, but sensing very clearly the conservative overtones, Gutzkow sought to replace it in the hearts and minds of the German people with a novel that would emphasize more the individual's commitment to the progressive forces in society and less the need to preserve and to learn from the achievements of the past. Instead of a single hero, concerned, to Gutzkow's mind, with relatively selfish, personal problems, he would describe a society of enlightened men, united in the lofty struggle for reform and social progress. In the place of the confused and despairing conservatism depicted in *Die Epigonen* by his contemporary, Immermann, he would champion radicalism and a firm commitment to marshaling the forces for change.

For Stifter, neither the desperate conservatism of Immermann nor the optimistic radicalism of Gutzkow represents an acceptable answer to the central question concerning the relationship of the moral individual to a changing, troubled time. Though Stifter, like Immermann, knew nostalgia for the age that was past and felt that the present represented a retrogression from the age of Goethe and Schiller, his strong commitment to the ideas of the Enlightenment prevented him from sharing Immermann's vision of the inevitable decline of European culture. Similarly, though the optimistic heritage from the Enlightenment might have inclined him favorably toward a program of change such as the one outlined by the Young German Gutzkow, Stifter was much too close to

---

[3] See Edward McInnes, „Zwischen Wilhelm Meister und Die Ritter vom Geist: zur Auseinandersetzung zwischen Bildungsroman und Sozialroman im 19. Jahrhundert," *Deutsche Vierteljahrsschrift für Literaturwissenschaft und Geistesgeschichte,* 43 (1969), 503.

Goethe in his veneration of the cultural heritage of Europe to countenance Gutzkow's reckless attitude toward the past. [4] Stifter's *Nachsommer* may be seen as an attempt to reconcile the extreme positions represented in the two novels by Immermann and Gutzkow and, in the tradition of the *Bildungsroman*, to enable the moral hero in the end to accept and play a positive role in his troubled time. But before we can proceed with an investigation of our particular concern with Stifter's *Bildungsroman* we must look more closely at his understanding of the dilemma facing the contemporary *Bildungsroman* hero, or, in other words, we must examine Stifter's understanding of the drift and import of the events of his own time as reflected in the novel. [5]

Although Austria, through the middle of the nineteenth century, had been spared the more drastic effects of the Industrial Revolution that was transforming society in the countries to the west, Stifter shared with the majority of contemporary European novelists the belief that the most significant aspect of European

---

[4] Of course for Stifter this cultural heritage meant more specifically and immediately than for Goethe also a Christian or religious heritage. It has been noted that the Young Germans hoped to see the theories that had been elaborated in the eighteenth century translated into deed and reality in the nineteenth. See, for example, Eitel Wolf Dobert, *Karl Gutzkow und seine Zeit*, (Bern and Munich: Francke Verlag, 1968), p. 64: „Was seit der Aufklärung Theorie geblieben war, sollte nun verwirklicht werden." It should also be noted that for the Young Germans, as so often for the essentially ahistorical Enlightenment, the past was useful chiefly as an example of error and ignorance.

[5] Since Goethe's introduction in *Wilhelm Meister* of a specifically contemporary element in the conflict between the moral individual and his imperfect society, the central issue in the *Bildungsroman* has been treated as one that is better expressed in historical than in universal terms, the hero becoming a representative of a specific social or economic class in a more or less specific period of European history, or, in the case of *Glasperlenspiel*, of pseudo-history.

society was dynamism.[6] Stifter saw a society in transition. A new age was being born, one which Stifter believed would ultimately witness great strides toward the perfection of human society. [7] Despite his underlying optimism, however, Stifter saw that the dynamism of the present gave no guarantee that changes would always be for the better. In fact, Stifter expected many setbacks during the critical age of transition. In the tumult of the present many things will be lost or forgotten that will be needed and sorely missed later. For Stifter, then, the present is characterized, not, as Immermann saw it, by incontestable and irreversible retrogression, nor, as Gutzkow would have it, by unqualified progress, but by great though often blind and misdirected activity.

The image that Stifter evokes several times in *Der Nachsommer* to convey his vision of his time—that of a tempest or a storm, but one that will surely be followed by a period of clear skies[8]—provides the larger context in which the idyllic serenity of the

---

[6] We must, of course, search carefully among the many long descriptive passages in *Nachsommer* to discover references to this dynamism. Stifter was no Balzac. He was interested primarily in showing what society could or should be, far less in depicting it as it is.

[7] Stifter's commitment to progress, not just individual progress, but social progress, is plainly indicated by several explicit statements by Risach in *Nachsommer*. This, and subsequent references to *Nachsommer* are to *Adalbert Stifter, Der Nachsommer*, ed. Max Stefl (Basel: Benno Schwabe & Co., 154). See. For example, p. 119, where Risach tells Heinrich: „Wenn die Fruchtbarkeit, wie sie durch Jahrzehnte in der Naturwissenschaft gewesen ist, durch Jahrhunderte anhält, so können wir gar nicht ahnen, wie weit es kommen wird. Nur das eine wissen wir jetzt, daß das noch unbebaute Feld unendlich größer ist als das bebaute." Risach develops this theme more explicitly later, pp. 520-21.

[8] See *Nachsommer*, p. 521: „Das Brausen, von welchem ich sprach, wird noch stärker werden, wie lange es dauern wird, welche übel entstehen werden, vermag ich nicht zu sagen; aber es wird eine Abklärung folgen, .

Rosenhaus and the *Sternenhof* must be viewed and is essential to the understanding of the novel. Stifter has been accused, even in his own day, of failing to come to terms with the pressing issues of the present. His *Nachsommer* seems to counsel a retreat from the turmoil of contemporary society for rather selfish reasons. Anticipating some of our own conclusions, however, we notice that because of the image of the storm—which will someday subside—there is something more positive in Heinrich's seeking shelter in the *Rosenhaus* at the beginning of Stifter's novel than there was at the end of Immermann's novel, in Hermann's desperate effort to hold out a while against an inevitable change for the worse. And again, because of the storm imagery—evidence that Stifter was sensitive to the elemental nature of the forces that were transforming society—there is something more than emotional conservatism in his opposition to the program for change optimistically championed by the Young Germans.

****

To many, the turbulent age in which Stifter set his idyllic *Rosenhaus*, or more accurately, in which *Der Nachsommer* was published, seemed to call for deeds, not contemplation, for an active commitment to society, not self-cultivation. The coolness with which Germany received *Nachsommer* upon its publication may be explained in part by the fact, just referred to, that in this novel Stifter seemed little concerned with the pressing issues of the day. The misunderstanding on this point was something that Stifter had clearly foreseen. He was resigned to being misunderstood by

---

. . . eine Zeit der Größe kommen, die in der Geschichte noch nicht dagewesen ist."

his age as he felt Goethe had been misunderstood by his own.[9] With Goethe he believed that in a disordered time the individual best serves society who, rather than tossing himself recklessly into the fray, seeks to discover and cultivate his natural inclinations and abilities; who, in other words, concerns himself with his own *Bildung*.

In the first chapter of *Nachsommer* Stifter takes those to task who would level the charge of social irresponsibility at him. Heinrich remarks that his father had exposed himself to the criticism of his colleagues by his decision to educate his son to be a "scientist in general," a rather dilettantish calling, they felt, which could be pursued only at the expense of a socially useful bourgeois occupation.[10] To this objection, however, Heinrich's father answers that a man has a primary obligation to himself, to self-discovery and self-fulfillment, and that the man who best meets his first obligation will better meet his second obligation, the one with respect to society.[11] More specifically, Heinrich's father argues that

---

[9] In the *Nachwort* to this edition of *Nachsommer*, p. 849, Max Stefl quotes from a letter by Stifter: „. . . und dann wird dieses Werk wie noch so viele bessere auf eine Zeit untergehen. Haben ja Goethes größte Werke . . . Deutschland kalt gelassen, es ist natürlich: Was höher als die Welt ist wird von ihr geschmäht, es bleibt aber doch, und siegt, wie Goethe überall gesiegt hat."

[10] See *Nachsommer*, I, p. 14: nicht die Ungeheuerlichkeit, welche in diesem Beginnen lag, war es, was die Leute meinem Vater übel nahmen, sondern sie sagten, er hätte mir einen Stand, der der bürgerlichen Gesellschaft nützlich ist, befehlen sollen, damit ich demselben meine Zeit und mein Leben widme, und einmal mit dem Bewußtsein scheiden könne, meine Schuldigkeit getan zu haben."

[11] *Nachsommer*, p. 14: Risach repeats this conviction toward the end of the novel, p. 704: „Ich wiederhole, was wir oft gesagt haben, und womit Euer ehrwürdiger Vater auch übereinstimmt, daß der Mensch seinen Lebensweg seiner selbst willen zur vollständigen Erfüllung seiner Kräfte wählen soll. Dadurch dient er auch dem Ganzen am besten."

precisely those men who have been most diligent in discovering and cultivating their own natural inclinations are most frequently the ones who render the most useful service to their countries in time of need.[12] He does not hide his contempt for those who claim to pursue their bourgeois occupation solely for the benefit of society,[13] a claim that lies near the center of a novel which, unlike Stifter's, enjoyed immense popularity in the nineteenth century—Gustav Freytag's *Soll und Haben*.

For Stifter, as for Goethe, the self-discovery and self-cultivation necessary to realize an individual's potential are possible only under ideal conditions and in a certain isolation from society. Society inhibits individual self-realization to the extent that it

---

[12]*Nachsommer*, I, 15: "Und aus solchen Männern, welche ihren innern Zug am weitesten ausgebildet, seien auch in Zeiten der Gefahr am öftesten die Helfer und die Retter ihres Vaterlandes hervorgegangen."

[13] *Nachsommer*, pp. 15-16: „Es gibt solche, die sagen, sie seien zum Wohle der Menschheit Kaufleute, Ärzte, Staatsdiener geworden; aber in den meisten Fällen ist es nicht wahr. Wenn nicht der innere Beruf sie dahin gezogen hat, so verbergen sie durch ihre Aussage nur einen schlechteren Grund, nämlich daß sie den Stand als ein Mittel betrachten, sich Geld und Gut und Lebensunterhalt zu erwerben. Oft sind sie auch, ohne weiter über eine Wahl mit sich zu Rate zu gehen, in den Stand geraten oder durch Umstände in ihn gestoßen worden, und nehmen das Wohl der Menschheit in den Mund, das sie bezweckt hätten, um nicht ihre Schwache zu gestehen. Dann ist noch eine eigene Gattung, welche immer von dem öffentlichen Wohle spricht. Das sind die, welche mit ihren eigenen Angelegenheiten in Unordnung sind. Sie geraten stets in Nöten, haben stets Ärger und Unannehmlichkeiten, und zwar aus ihrem eigenen Leichtsinne: und da liegt es ihnen als Ausweg neben der Hand, den öffentlichen Zuständen für ihre Lage schuld zu geben, und zu sagen, sie waren eigentlich recht auf das Vaterland bedacht, und sie würden alles am besten in demselben einrichten. Aber wenn wirklich die Lage kommt, daß das Vaterland sie beruft, so geht es dem Vaterlande, wie es früher ihren eigenen Angelegenheiten gegangen ist."

requires early specialization, which leads to one-sidedness—a problem that the young Wilhelm Meister had clearly recognized. Stifter admits that there is a practical, economic side to the question, but he believes that the short-term considerations are greatly outweighed by the long-term implications of the neglect of the whole personality.[14]

Stifter's idea as to what actually constitutes ideal conditions for the natural development of the human personality corresponds, with certain key differences to be taken up later, very closely to Goethe's idea in *Wilhelm Meister*. For Stifter, as for Goethe,[15] it is important that the developing personality be sheltered from too direct or violent influences, as any strong or one-sided influence could easily lead the impressionable personality in a direction

---

[14] Thus Risach tells Heinrich, *Nachsommer*, p. 704: „Unsere gesellschaftlichen Verhältnisse sind so geworden, daß zur Befriedigung unserer stofflichen Bedürfnisse ein sehr großer Aufwand gehört. Daher werden junge Leute, ehe sie sich selber bewußt werden, in Laufbahnen gebracht, die ihnen den Erwerb dessen, was sie zur Befriedigung der angeführten Bedürfnisse brauchen, sichern. Von einem Berufe ist da nicht die Rede. Das ist schlimm, sehr schlimm, und die Menschheit wird dadurch immer mehr eine Herde. Wo noch eine Wahl möglich ist, weil man nicht nach sogenanntem Broterwerbe auszugehen braucht, dort sollte man sich seiner Kräfte sehr klar bewußt werden, ehe man ihnen den Wirkungskreis zuteilt. Aber muß man nicht in der Jugend wählen, weil es sonst zu spät ist? Und kann man sich in der Jugend immer seiner Kraft bewußt werden? Es ist schwierig, und mögen, die beteiligt sind, darüber wachen, daß weniger leichtsinnig verfahren werde." Note the echo from Immermann's *Epigonen*, note 2: „. . . künstliche Bedürfnisse künstlich zu befriedigen."

[15] That is, to the extent that we may equate Goethe's educational theories with those of the Abbé and the *Oheim*. Goethe, characteristically, maintains a certain ironic distance from his characters. See Lucács, pp. 83-84.

contrary to its own inner inclination.[16] The activity of the true pedagogue is limited almost completely to the creation of an environment in which discovery and self-realization may take place.[17] The only type of personal influence that he may exert on his charge is the gentle influence of example and companionship. For Stifter, as for Goethe, the crucial word is *Umgang*.[18]

An important way in which Stifter's conception of the ideal environment for the natural development of the human personality differs from Goethe's is observable in a subtle but significant shift in the role of works of art in the total picture. In Risach's *Rosenhaus*, as is in the *Oheim*'s castle, the art treasures

---

[16] Thus Heinrich's father withholds the reading of Shakespeare and the visiting of the theater from his son until he can be sure that his son's personality has developed to such a point that it will not be completely dominated by these powerful influences, sparing him the fate of Wilhelm Meister. *Nachsommer*, pp. 187-88.

[17] The extensive plant imagery in this novel serves, among other things, to underline the nature of this pedagogical activity, which is really a kind of cultivation. Thus the educator/gardner Risach may take elaborate precautions and care to prepare the ground and to create and maintain an ideal environment, but in the end it is the individual—the rose or the cactus, the *Schöne Seele,* Natalie or Heinrich Drendorf—which develops according to its own internal inclination and laws toward self-realization.

[18] Thus Mathilde's father told the young Risach, *Nachsommer*, p. 723: „Erziehung ist wohl nichts als Umgang." Risach repeats this conviction to Heinrich's father, p. 816: „Ich muß antworten wie bei Natalien, ‚erwiderte mein Gastfreund, ‚sein selbst hat sich entwickelt, und aller Umgang, der ihm zu Teil geworden, vorerst der Eurige, hat geholfen.'" See also Emil Staiger, *Adalbert Stifter als Dichter der Ehrfurcht* (Heidelberg: Lothar Stiehm Verlag, 1967), p. 28: „Freilich spricht Stifter seine Gesetze nicht in abstrakter Weise, sondern in Anschaulichen Vorbildern aus, seiner Ansicht gemäß, daß alle echte Erziehung Umgang sei. Der Jüngling Heinrich Drendorf geht mit schönen Menschen und Dingen um und entfaltet so seinen eigenen Wert."

figure prominently. For the classicist Goethe the work of art was a quasi-mystical concept, autonomous and absolute. By the middle of the nineteenth century the classical (and even the related romantic concept of art) had fallen into considerable disrepute in many circles. Thus, the *Epigone*, Stifter, writing in an increasingly materialistic age, could presuppose little real sympathy for his essentially classical conception of art. It was necessary for him to re-educate the reader and to convince him of the inherent worth and importance of art. In his *Nachsommer* the work of art emerges as a special category of the *thing*,[19] and its value for the person who has learned to appreciate it is that it helps him see deeper into the nature of things.

Stifter's emphasis on the importance of contact with and study of things in general—as opposed to Goethe's greater stressing of the importance of art works—is conditioned by his concern with growing interest among his contemporaries in material acquisitions. It must have been a source of profound dismay to our Austrian poet that precisely in an age of materialism the material thing itself and the material world, the world of nature, should receive so little objective recognition. People tend to judge things, Stifter believed, as important or unimportant, valuable or worthless according to whether or not they happen to be objects of their passions.[20] But this emphasis on the importance of things also

---

[19] An important concept for Stifter which we cannot discuss in detail here. See Wilhelm Dehn, *Ding und Vernunft* (Bonn: H. Bouvier und Co., 1969), for discussions of „Der Ding-Begriff und Stifters Sprachgebrauch," „Wesenheit der Dinge," and „Forderung der Dinge."

[20] Thus Risach tells Heinrich, *Nachsommer*, I, 213: „. . . wenn ein Übermaß von Wunsche nun Begehrungen in uns ist, so hören wir nur diese immer an, und vermögen nicht die Unschuld der Dinge außer uns zu fassen. Leider heißen wir sie wichtig, wenn sie Gegenstände unserer Leidenschaften sind, und unwichtig, wenn sie zu diesen in keinen Beziehungen stehen, während es doch oft umgekehrt sein kann."

reflects Stifter's rejection of the thesis that Man is the measure of all things [21] —the one aspect of the classical heritage that his contemporaries seemed willing to accept—and thus betrays a measure of departure from the ideas of German classicism that Stifter may not have recognized. From a dispassionate study of things in his youth and throughout his life a man learns of his inherently modest and dependent position in the universe, and of the way to secure and fill that position.

On a very important level the story of Heinrich's education, the story of the securing and the development of his personality up to the point where he may play an effective role in society—*wirken*—is the account of his growing orientation in the world of nature and of human institutions. [22] This orientation proceeds according to the workings of a gentle dialectic which causes him to move in an ever widening arc from a study of natural phenomena to a study of art objects, which in turn provides him with new insights and a new basis for the further understanding of the laws and order underlying both the things of nature and human development, relationships and institutions. Thus when Heinrich first arrives at the *Rosenhaus* he has progressed only so far in his orientation from the study of nature that he can begin to appreciate the most thing-like or natural art objects, such as buildings and their furnishings. Risach therefore makes no effort

---

[21]Compare Emil Staiger, *Adalbert Stifter als Dichter der Ehrfurcht*, p. 26: „Bei Stifter aber ist nicht der Mensch das Maß der Dinge, sondern Gott."
[22] It is thus of some symbolic significance that Heinrich becomes a surveyor. We might note here that the ability to *wirken*, which in both *Agathon* and *Wilhelm Meister* was a test, of sorts, of personality, is also a test of orientation. A person who does not know where he stands, both literally and figuratively, will find it impossible to act meaningfully and effectively.

to call Heinrich's attention to his most valuable art treasures.[23]
From his study of the natural art objects, his host guides him to that
of sketches of such natural art works—a gentle step away from the
study of craftsmanship and applied art in the direction of *pure* art.[24]
But by studying, first, a portfolio containing sketches of buildings,
and then a second one containing sketches of furnishings and
implements (*Geräte*) Heinrich learns more about the things
themselves. He learns, for example, something about the nature of
architecture, which is a sort of *Bildung* or purposeful shaping of

---

[23] Heinrich later understands and appreciates the patience and
indulgence of his *Gastfreund, Nachsommer*, p. 414: „Ich machte also jetzt
die Erfahrung, daß in früherer Zeit, da ich mein Augenmerk noch weniger
auf Gemälde und ähnliche Kunstwerke gerichtet hatte, und dieselben
einen tiefen Platz in meinem Innern noch nicht einnahmen, mich
geschont habe, daß man nicht eingegangen sei, in meiner Gegenwart von
den in dem Hause befindlichen Kunstwerken zu sprechen, um mich nicht
in einen Kreis zu nötigen, der in jenem Augenblicke noch beinahe
außerhalb meiner Seelenkräfte lag. Mir kam jetzt auch zu Sinne, daß in
gleicher Weise mein Vater nie zu mir auf eigenen Antrieb von seinen
Bildern gesprochen habe, und daß er sich nur in so weit über dieselben
eingelassen, als ich selber darauf zu sprechen kam."

[24] See *Nahsommer*, I, 97-104. Emil Staiger, Stifter, p. 30, emphasizes the
intimate relationship that exists for Stifter between things and works of
art: „Da der Mensch sich so an einen bescheidenen Platz zurückgestellt
sieht, daß er es sich versagen muß, als Krone der Schöpfung gelten zu
wollen, ziemt es sich nicht, die Betrachtung der Welt mit der von dem
Idealismus gestellten Frage ‚Was ist der Mensch' zu beginnen . . . .
Deshalb setzt die Betrachtung der Künste hier später ein als die der Natur.
Und der Weg beginnt von unten, beim Kunstgewerbe, ja beim Handwerk,
wo der übereilte, schwärmerische Künstler sich immer wieder von
seinem Stoff zurechtgewiesen sieht, wo er sich der Maserung der Holzer,
dem Geäder des Marmors, der Dichte des Silbers und des Goldes fügen
muß, wenn er gestalten will. Damit bleibt er vor Willkür bewahrt und
dämmert ihm schon früh die Ahnung, daß auch das künstlerische
Gestalten, wie das Bilden der Natur, Gesetzen unterworfen ist."

material toward a given end. And by observing that there is something in the form of the *Geräte* of a given era which corresponds to the architecture of the same period Heinrich learns something about the necessarily organic nature of *Bildung*, which must concern itself not only with narrowly defined ends, but with the totality.

Only toward the end of the novel has Heinrich progressed far enough in his dialectical advance between a study of things and a study of art to be able to appreciate the greatest works of art—symbolized by his *discovery* of the marble statue in the *Rosenhaus*. Only when Heinrich has reached the high level of insight and orientation indicated by his ability to appreciate such art is he ready to take up his calling, and only then is he ready for marriage with Natalie. In other words, only then is he ready to begin an effective and meaningful *Wirken* among men.

But in an age where, according to Stifter's analysis, even things are no longer viewed objectively, but only as they relate to individual passions and desires, there seems to be little basis for hope for the survival of art. Heinrich's *Bildung* must take place, therefore, as we already noted, in relative isolation from the present, in *castles*—epitomized by the *Rosenhaus*—which are, like the *Oheim*'s castle in the *Lehrjahre*, protective cultural vaults.

That, in Stifter's view, the situation within bourgeois society had deteriorated even beyond the stage noted by Goethe is suggested by Risach's concern not only with preserving works of art, but, perhaps more importantly, with restoring them before adding them to his collection. Almost everything that Risach keeps in the *Rosenhaus* has been restored or re-created under his watchful eye in the workshop of Master Eustache. The deterioration of the German middle class signaled in Goethe's novel by the sale of the art collection would now appear to be complete. The great collections have been broken up and scattered, and the bourgeoisie seems to have no memory of its—according to Goethe and Stifter—traditional role of creator and custodian of the arts and crafts.[25] Only isolated individuals of the bourgeoisie, like Risach and Heinrich's father, are still concerned with saving their cultural heritage, and their activities resemble more the painstaking work of the archeologist than the more leisured collecting of the *Oheim* in Goethe's novel. The chief function of the castle in *Nachsommer*, shifting, as it does, from a mission of preserving to a mission of restoring and re-creating, corresponds to the shift in emphasis we noted between *Agathon* and *Wilhelm Meister*, there, from a desire to preserve an endangered personality to the more pressing task of first obtaining one. In each instance the shift is toward a greater sense of urgency on the part of the later poet.

This last statement brings us back to a fact first mentioned in Chapter 2, namely that *Nachsommer* provided the only exception to a general rule that the *Bildungsroman* hero be an orphan figure or an outsider. Since the *Bildungsroman* may be regarded as a development of the picaresque novel, and since *Nachsommer* is an important element in the *Bildungsroman* tradition, part of Heinrich's education might well be expected to include a picaresque experience of his imperfect society. The absence of any such experience is best explained if *Nachsommer* is viewed as standing in a close and complementary relationship to Goethe's *Wilhelm Meister*.

---

[25] Thus, even in the most positive picture that we have of mid-nineteenth-century German bourgeoisie, from Freytag's *Soll und Haben*, which appeared just two years before Stifter's *Nachsommer*, it is precisely those things for which Wilhelm's father had foolishly bartered the art collection—capital for his business and costly furnishing for his house—that are the symbols and guarantors of worth and permanence.

As stated above, Stifter was not concerned with painting a picture of society as it actually was—a task which he gladly left to Immermann and Gutzkow. It was enough for his purposes to refer simply to the realities of his day, realities which he conspicuously omits from the isolated microcosm of the *Rosenhaus*. Similarly, Stifter must have felt that it was not necessary to restate the conflict between the moral individual and contemporary society, as this conflict had been clearly formulated by Goethe in the *Lehrjahre*. The most convincing part of Goethe's novel, we noted, was the realistic first part, the first five books, which contain Wilhelm's experience of contemporary society. The reconciliation of a disillusioned Wilhelm to his society was handled somewhat less satisfactorily in the later, stylized chapters. In other words, in Goethe's novel we experience Wilhelm's conflict with his society in such a way that we do not experience the resolution of this conflict, which we merely see or hear about. In *Nachsommer* Stifter attempts to let us experience the resolution of a conflict, which, in contrast, is merely referred to.

The recounting of Risach's story—*Der Rückblick*—is the only part of the long novel that contains anything like the picaresque experience of society by the hero of a *Bildungsroman*.[26] Risach's adventure, the story of his missed vocation, is offered as an explanation for the extraordinary precautions that are taken with Heinrich. So that there will be no misunderstanding the intent of the story, Risach, in a few anticipatory remarks at the end of the preceding chapter, places the blame for such personal tragedies largely on conditions within society.[27]

---

[26] Compare Staiger, *Stifter*, p. 28: „Man pflegt es einen Roman zu nennen. Romanhaft aber sind nur die wenigsten Seiten, die von der Jugend des Freiherrn von Risach berichten."

[27] See note 14 above. In the story itself, self-willed passion, to Stifter's mind always destructive, clearly bears some of the blame in the case of

Since only Risach's story contains an element of conflict with contemporary society, it is clearly misleading to compare Heinrich with the heroes of the earlier *Bildungsromane*. Risach, it would seem, is not only the main character in the novel—he is also the true *Bildungsroman* hero, the orphan and outsider who finds his way home. Heinrich's conflictless development contrasts with Risach's trying experience of contemporary society much in the same way that Lothario's ideal development contrasts with Wilhelm's confused flight from the *emptiness* of his bourgeois home.[28] But whereas the story of Lothario's education under the ideal influences of the *Oheim* and his castle is related only second-hand, largely through incidental remarks made by the *Schöne Seele*, Heinrich's education under similarly ideal conditions takes place before the reader's eyes and forms the bulk of the novel. Conversely, whereas Wilhelm's picaresque experience of his society forms the bulk of the *Lehrjahre*, Risach's essentially similar brush with real life is related only second-hand, through Heinrich, and it forms only a small fraction of the whole novel. It would seem thus that in *Nachsommer* Stifter has—with reference to Goethe's

---

Mathilde and Risach. That is, Stifter thinks that precautions are necessary with the young not only because of conditions within society but also because of the human condition.

[28] Since we concluded in Chapter 4 that it is more appropriate to view Lothario rather than Wilhelm Meister as the most direct literary descendant of Agathon, it would now appear that there is a closer link between *Rococo* Wieland and *Biedermeier* Stifter than is normally felt to exist. The comparison between Lothario, the Faustian nobleman, and Heinrich Drendorf, the retiring, self-effacing merchant's son, may seem, at first glance, to be quite far-fetched. But when we remember that we should compare the Lothario we meet in Book 7 of the *Lehrjahre* not with Heinrich in the process of becoming, but with the mature, self-confident, cultured scientist who emerges at the end of the novel, then the comparison does not seem quite so far-fetched.

analysis of the factors involved—attempted to give us his idea of all that actually goes into the formation of a self-confident, energetic, whole, moral character such as Lothario.[29]

Stifter's shift away from emphasis on exposing the problem to a greater stress on elaborating the solution corresponds to the shift we noted in the function of the castle in *Nachsommer,* which must serve not only as a repository for art treasures like the *Oheim's* castle, but also as a workshop in which the decaying relics are restored or re-created. Just as Risach found it necessary to restore with painstaking attention to detail the art treasures that he will preserve in his collection, so must Stifter spend most of his energies in an effort to re-create the atmosphere and the conditions in which—according to his view—ideal education may take place.

In view of the large measure of misunderstanding and even hostility with which *Nachsommer* was received in the nineteenth century, and with which it continues to be regarded by a large number of critics today, it seems necessary to examine further the genuineness, if not the validity, of Stifter's paradoxical view that the individual, even in the time of crisis, must first serve himself to be able to serve best the deepest needs of his society. In other words, to what extent can *Nachsommer* be regarded as a true *Bildungsroman*? To what extent does this novel offer a positive solution to the moral hero's conflict with his society, or, to what extent might it justly be considered a skirting of pressing social problems? To what extent is *Nachsommer* a mere escapist dream?

Answers to these questions may be found by a closer look at the role of the various castles in the novel. The true *Bildungsroman* castle, we remember, serves a negative and a positive function

---

[29] The reader should not start at the thought of the libertine Lothario as a moral hero—we remember from our discussion in Chapter 2 that the *Bildungsroman* hero is a moral hero, and that his commitment to the betterment of his society is a moral commitment.

with respect to society. In *Nachsommer*, the negative function of the castle, that of protecting and nurturing, seems to receive exaggerated stress in comparison with the stress given the assertion that Heinrich must devote himself to his own development to be enabled to serve society's needs. Horst Brunner specifically referred to the *Rosenhaus* in his discussion of quasi-islands,[30] thereby suggesting the absolute (as opposed to the ambivalent) nature of Risach's Alpine retreat. We need more evidence, it would seem, of a positive function of this castle with respect to society, evidence that it is actually more than just a quasi-island retreat; that it is, in fact, a true *Bildungsroman* castle.

Risach himself offers early evidence during Heinrich's first visit to the *Rosenhaus*, when he explains his reasons for attracting songbirds to his orchard. He remarks on the difficulty of convincing his neighbors of the need for reforms and improvements in their methods of husbandry. It is useless, he notes, to try to reason with these practical men. One can reach them only by showing them, by making an example of one's own estate.[31] Later on he says of his model farmhouse, „Wenn man mehrere Beispiele aufstellte, so würden sich im Lande die Ansichten über das notwendige Aussehen und die Wohnbarkeit der Häuser ändern. *Dieses Haus soll ein Beispiel sein.*"[32] Another of the castles, Mathilde's *Sternenhof*, is depicted as having already effected some changes in the vicinity through the power of example.[33] In relating his story to Heinrich, Risach sums up his reasons for retreating to the country as follows:

---

[30]Brunner, *Die poetische Insel*, p. 28.
[31]*Nachsommer*, pp. 164-65: „'[sie] sind . . . schwer zu bewegen, weil sie meinen, es gehe nicht. Wir müssen ihnen aber zeigen, daß es geht.'"
[32]*Nachsommer*, p. 221 (emphasis added).
[33]*Nachsommer*, p. 417.

> Ich hatte die Absicht, mir für die letzten Tage meines Lebens einen Landsitz zu gründen, und dort einigen wissenschaftlichen Arbeiten, einigen Genüsse der Kunst, so weit ich dazu fähig wäre, der Bewirtschaftung meiner Felder und Gärten, und hie und da *einer gemeinnützigen Maß Regel für die Umgebung zu leben.*[34]

And finally, Risach challenges Heinrich's father late in the novel to a contest, to see which of them „mit geringerem Aufwande seinen Sitz zu einem größeren Kunstwerke machen kann."[35] Whereas men like the reformer Gutzkow might regard such an undertaking as a rather anti-social misallocation of talent and resources, for Stifter it represented a response to a pressing social problem. His present, as we noted, was, according to Stifter's view, characterized by misdirected or directionless dynamism. What is needed is not more action, not deeds, Stifter thought, but orientation, direction, a beacon in the storm. By making their lives and their estates into works of art, Stifter believed, Risach and the elder Drendorf were becoming such beacons, and thus were actually serving the most pressing need of their society.

To accuse Stifter of ignoring the pressing needs of his world is to deny him his own opinion as to what the problems actually were. Today it is less easy to be sure that Stifter was wrong in insisting above all else on the organic nature of change. The current recognition of an ecological crisis is a tacit admission of the rightness of Stifter's insistence on the relatively modest, dependent position of man in the hierarchy of the universe, on his need to orient himself in his environment before attempting to alter it. Stifter's insistence on the necessity of Man's working with nature—a good example of which is Risach's use of songbirds to control the insects in his orchard—an idea directly opposed to the

---

[34]*Nachsommer*, p. 773. (Emphasis added).
[35]*Nachsommer*, p. 826.

nineteenth-century scientist's dream of conquering nature, would meet with the hearty approbation from the majority of scientists today.

Stifter was a man profoundly torn by two opposing elemental forces, the force for change and the force which resists change, a man more profoundly torn than any of the Young Germans or the earlier writers of *Bildungsromane*. His own *Bildungsroman* is the record of his attempt to reconcile these opposing forces by discovering a process of organic change, of becoming, which is based solely on being, on the nature and essence of the universe. This attempt is symbolized most adequately, perhaps, by the configuration of the most important *Bildungsroman* castle in *Nachsommer*, the *Rosenhaus*, which, in its relative isolation from contemporary society, is closed with respect to arbitrary or chaotic change, but which is completely open with respect to the organic change of the universe.[36]

In a certain sense the tradition of the *Bildungsroman* that began with Wieland's *Agathon* culminates in Stifter's *Nachsommer*. As we shall see in the next section, Keller's *Der Grüne Heinrich*, while it is more than superficially related to this German tradition, has deep roots in an experience that is essentially alien to the one that produced the *Bildungsroman*. Likewise, as we shall see in the concluding chapter, Mann's *Zauberberg* and Hesse's *Glasperlenspiel* are actually more sentimental than naïve elements in this tradition.

---

[36] Thus Risach gently rebukes Heinrich for promising to preserve the estate unchanged after the death of the older man, *Nachsommer*, p. 836.

Keller's *Der Grüne Heinrich*

At the beginning of this chapter we argued that the resemblance of Stifter's *Bildungsroman* to Goethe's, in the most important aspects of theme and structure is, to a large extent a reflection of the two poets' basically similar relationship to their respective eras. Stifter's reaction to the March Revolution of 1848, which he viewed from the perspective of the anachronistic Austrian order, corresponds to Goethe's reaction to the French Revolution some sixty years before. The ways in which Gottfried Keller's *Der Grüne Heinrich*[37] differs from the *Bildungsromane* of Goethe and Stifter are, to a considerable extent, a reflection of the Swiss poet's basically different experience of his time.[38] Moreover, Keller's +experience of his time is reflected, as we would expect, in the configuration and the function of the *Bildungsroman* castles in *Der Grüne Heinrich.*

If the literary historian is ever justified in calling attention to the relationship that exists between a poet's works and his experience of his time, his vision of his society—and for the *Bildungsroman* such a procedure is called for—then he is doubly justified in doing so in the case of Gottfried Keller. The corpus of Keller's work is inseparable from his vision of the history and the potentialities of

---

[37] Unless otherwise stated, all references to *Der Grüne Heinrich* are to its second or revised form. See Jonas Frankel, *Gottfried Keller: Sämtliche Werke*, Vols. III-VI (Erlengach-Zürich and Munich: Eugen Rentsch Verlag, 1926).

[38] We remember from Chapter 2, p. 28, that Keller's *Der Grüne Heinrich* offers the only exception to the rule that the *Bildungsroman* hero be a *type*, like the picaresque hero. This exception, we felt, might, in view of Keller's non-German citizenship, provide a clue for a further definition of the *Bildungsroman*. As we shall see below, this exception, this difference, is closely related to Keller's exceptional, non-German experience of his time.

the energetic, democratic Swiss people, and his sense of responsibility to this people as a writer and poet.[39]

The image of Switzerland that emerges in Keller's works, that
of something unique and something special in European history,
has deep roots in geo-political reality. The mountainous little
republic with its legendary independence and rather liberal institutions is something of an anomaly in monarchial, imperial, or even
revolutionary Europe. Like Germany, Switzerland's central location
makes it a meeting place and a crossroads for Europe. But unlike
Germany, where open borders to the West, the North, and the East
offer a constant invitation to invasion and conquest, the
mountainous terrain of most of Switzerland tends to protect the
little republic from dangers that threaten from without.
Switzerland, in fact, is a sort of *Bildungsroman* castle itself, which
offers its people not only contact with the larger society of Europe,
but also a judicious amount of isolation from that society. Indeed,
Keller thought of Switzerland in such terms—without, naturally,
using the terminology of this thesis— a fact which will become
clearer as we proceed in this investigation. We note now merely
that Keller was careful to record Heinrich's leaving and re-entering
the castle of Switzerland, and that his picaresque or disillusioning
experience of society occurs not in Switzerland, but outside, in
Germany.

****

---

[39] Compare Lucács, p. 364: „Die Kellersche Utopie in Bezug auf die
Schweiz besteht nur darin, daß er glaubt, diesem Leben wohne die Kraft
inne, die inneren gesellschafttlichen Bedrohungen von sich aus zu
überwinden."

More than either Goethe or Stifter, Keller is a conscious representative of the Enlightenment.[40] For a brief period the young Keller was closely associated with the radical inheritors of this tradition, the Young Germans. The mature Keller, however, like Goethe, and like his own contemporary to the east, Stifter, believed that any meaningful changes in society must be the result of organic evolution. But, at least at the writing of *Der Grüne Heinrich*, he differed from Goethe and Stifter in that he believed that the changes of his day represented such an organic process—at least in Switzerland.[41] Swiss society, for Keller, is *Innenraum*, to use

---

[40] See Herbert W. Reichert, *Basic Concepts in the Philosophy of Gottfried Keller*, University of North Carolina Studies in the Germanic Languages and Literatures, No. 1 (Chapel Hill: The University of North Carolina Press, 1949), p. 25: "Man's destiny, Keller felt, was especially guided by the law of time. With the philosophic optimism of the preceding century, Keller believed that man was evolving, inevitably driven by natural law, to perfection." And p. 39: "Keller became . . . intensely interested in the means to moral freedom, namely enlightenment." Also pp. 47/48: "He became more and more convinced that prejudice, preconception and misunderstanding were the root of all evil, and became increasingly certain that *enlightenment* was the sole panacea for man's ills. And with his optimistic faith in *inevitable progress*, his conviction became ever greater that the goal of mankind was precisely intellectual freedom . . . The greatest sin imaginable was skepticism regarding man's perfectibility" (emphasis added). See also Lukacs, p. 364: „Die bürgerliche Tüchtigkeit bei Keller ist eine gedanklich-moralische Weiterführung der Ethik der Aufklärung." And p. 369: „Keller ist als Schriftsteller ein ebenso überzeugter Aufklärer, wie es etwa Diderot oder Lessing waren."

[41] Thus Heinrich notes, upon his return from Germany, *Der Grüne Heinrich*, VI, p. 283: „Als ich den Rhein überschritt und das Land betrat, was dieses gerade mit dem Getöse jener politischen Aktionen erfüllt, welche mit dem Umwandlungsprozesse eines fünfhundert jährigen Staatenbundes in einen Bundestaat abschlossen, ein organischer Prozeß, . . .," See also Lukacs, p. 342: „Die deutsche Freiheitsdichtung der vierziger Jahre wirkte stark auf den jungen Keller … Seine Eigenart besteht darin,

Brunner's terminology, and corresponds to the sheltered, castle environment of the earlier *Bildungsromane*. It is not something against which the hero must be protected, rather it is precisely the environment in which he must live, experience, and develop. Keller's criticism of Swiss society is the warm-hearted criticism of the insider, and there is never a serious question of the value and necessity of the daily give-and-take of the social experience in an essentially healthy society—a radical departure from the pessimism of an Immermann or even Stifter.

The fact that Heinrich is initially an outsider with respect to his society seems to militate against this interpretation. [42] The picaresque perspective of the outsider, we remember, is a critical or satirical perspective, and Keller does use this perspective for directing some criticism at Swiss society and institutions, especially at the system of public schools. But there is an important difference between the outsider position of Heinrich and the more truly picaresque perspective of Wilhelm Meister. Whereas Wilhelm very consciously and deliberately flees to the periphery of his bourgeois society, Heinrich is banished quite against his will, and, like the lonely albeit resourceful Robinson on his isle, never really forgets his deplorable predicament.

The comparison with Robison Crusoe is illuminating. [43] Robinson, in his exile, is able as an outsider to view the society he

---

daß er die rückläufige Bewegung nach der Niederlage der Revolution nicht mitmacht. Davor bewahrt ihn die Schweizer Demokratie."

[42] Heinrich's position as an outsider with respect to his society during his early years is suggested by his name. See *Der Grüne Heinrich*, IV, 129: „. . . wie man mir überhaupt keine Schwierigkeiten machte, aus dem einfachen Grunde, weil ich der grüne Heinrich hieß, d.h., weil ich eine abgesonderte und abgeschiedene Erscheinung war."

[43] England, itself, is, like Switzerland, a sort of *Bildungsroman* castle. Although its island nature assures a certain isolation from the dangers of the continental society, such as war and invasion, England is close enough

left behind with considerable objectivity. It is a relatively easy thing for him in his daily struggle for survival to distinguish between the essential and the merely accidental, superfluous aspects of English social life. Through the figure of Robinson, Defoe is able to direct severe criticism at British society without ever suggesting that life in exile from this society is preferable to life within it. Similarly, Keller can be harshly critical of certain aspects of Swiss society without counseling even a partial withdrawal from that society. For at the heart of all his criticism is the assumption that intimate contact with society is essential for the normal, healthy development of the individual.[44] It is one of Heinrich's chief tasks to discover the essentially personal nature of his predicament, and then, like Robinson, to overcome it and to find his way back into his community.[45]

That Heinrich's outsider position with respect to his society does not serve the same thematic ends as does Wilhelm Meister's

---

to the continent to have plenty of contact with the main streams of European thought. The favorable situation of both Switzerland and England, the happy balance between contact with and isolation from European society, may go far in explaining why democratic institutions developed organically in these two countries, while such institutions had to be transplanted, sometimes violently, and often with little success, in less fortunate nations of Europe, such as France and Germany.

[44] See *Der Grüne Heinrich*, III, p. 192: „. . . denn ein Kind von der allgemeinen Erziehung ausschließen, heißt nichts anderes, als seine innere Entwicklung, sein geistiges Leben köpfen."

[45] Compare Lucács, pp. 394-95: „Im weitern führt Keller aus, daß wenn das gesellschaftliche Moment als Ursache des Scheiterns in den Vordergrund tritt, ein sozialer Tendenzroman entstehe, wenn hingegen die Schuld des einzelnen vorherrscht, das Werk einen moralischen Charakter erhalte: er selbst entscheide sich für den zweiten Weg. Die Erklärung Kellers ist eine unausgesprochene Polemik gegen die oberflächlichen Tendenzromane des ‚Jungen Deutschland.'"

conflict with his society is further suggested by the fact that Keller's hero possessed in his father a good model for an active, moral life in society. Wilhelm's estrangement from his father, we remember, is a sign of his estrangement from his society, for his father is representative of a good portion of the German bourgeoisie. Heinrich's love and respect for his father, on the other hand, is an equally clear sign of Heinrich's love and respect for his fatherland, for the elder Lee is the product and representative of the best elements of Swiss society.[46]

Keller is careful to indicate the connection between the death of Heinrich's father and the boy's subsequent alienation from society. Frau Lee is no Frau Regula Amrain, who could step in and be a father to her fatherless son. She is a good woman, but her limitations are clearly in evidence. Her inability, for example, to capture her son's imagination or satisfy his curiosity with the constant repetition of her favorite biblical tales is cited as one of the reasons for the fascination that Frau Margaret held for her son.[47] The influence that the *Trödelfrau* exerted on Heinrich is comparable to the exaggerated and misleading influence that the puppet theater was able to exert on Wilhelm Meister in his *empty* paternal home.[48] Like Wilhelm and the *Schöne Seele*, Heinrich had

---

[46] In other words, Heinrich's good relationship to his father, or to the memory of his father, is not explainable—as was Heinrich Drendorf's to his father—by the father's *exceptional* relationship to his society.

[47] *Der Grüne Heinrich*, III, pp. 57-58: „. . . so blieben mir doch die Phantasie und das Gemüt leer, solange ich keine neue Nahrung schöpfte, . . . Indessen hatte ich eine Freundschaft geschlossen, welche meiner suchenden Phantasie zu Hilfe kam."

[48] See *Der Grüne Heinrich*, IV, p. 88: „Mit all diesen Eindrücken beladen, zog ich dann über die Gasse wieder nach Hause und spann in der Stille unserer Stube den Stoff zu großen träumerischen Geweben aus, wozu die erregte Phantasie den Einschlag gab. Sie verflochten sich mir mit dem

too much opportunity for "Umgang mit sich selbst;"[49] he had an overdeveloped imagination that was much in need of the corrective influences that might have been his in the healthy ridicule and guidance of his self-confident father.[50]

Heinrich begins to experience a corrective influence during his first visit to his mother's native village, in the home of her brother—an obvious foster-father figure. Though not the energetic, active man that Heinrich's father was, this uncle is a representative of the healthy, still rural and small-town Swiss society. The contrast with the *Oheim* figures of *Wilhelm Meister* and *Nachsommer* is striking. Heinrich Lee's uncle represents no tradition or culture that does not form a real, alive, and working element of contemporary rural Swiss society. His dwelling place is not a "cultural vault," but merely the home of a rather educated

---

wirklichen Leben, daß ich sie kaum von demselben unterscheiden konnte."

[49]*Der Grüne Heinrich*, IV, p. 104: „Desto eifriger verkehrte ich im Stillen mit mir selbst, in der Welt, die ich mir zu bauen gezwungen war."

[50]Thus Heinrich observes, *Der Grüne Heinrich*, III, p. 236: „Menschen, welche etwas Besseres oder Tieferes ahnen und wünschen, werden sich, wie ich glaube, mehr und mehr aller lächerlichen Äußerlichkeiten enthalten, je mehr sie dem geahnten Wesen durch Erfahrung und Tat nahe treten; je weiter sie aber noch davon entfernt sind, desto mehr klammern sie sich an solche Schnörkeleien. Allein gerade diese Äußerlichkeit verhindert oft das Innere, sich rasch zu entwickeln, *wenn nicht ein Mann und Vater vorhanden ist, welcher sie mit gesundem Spotte beschneidet und unterdrückt*, indessen er dem aufstrebenden Sohne das Wahre mit fester Hand vorzeichnet." (Emphasis added). And later, VI, p. 4: „Zum ersten Male meines Erinnerns ward ich dieses Gefühls der Vaterlosigkeit deutlicher inne, und es wallte als ich mir rasch vergegenwärtigte, wie ich durch das Leben des Vaters der Frühen Freiheit beraubt, vielleicht gewaltsamer Zucht unterworfen, aber auch auf gesicherte Wege geführt worden wäre."

and well-to-do farmer, [51] completely open with respect to contemporary society, a center of village social life. Heinrich, who comes to the village with his head full of fantastic ideas, begins in the invigorating atmosphere of his uncle's home to see himself in a new light and to re-examine some of his assumptions.

Heinrich's decision to become a landscape painter antecedes this visit. A careful reading of the novel reveals that this idea was born of and nurtured by Heinrich's "eccentric" or peripheral position in society. It is significant, for example, that Heinrich's first interest in painting is attributed to the visit to his city of a troupe of actors.[52] Heinrich's conviction that he should become a painter is now strengthened by an uncritical, naïve reading of Gessner, a dusty volume of whose works he finds in his uncle's house, the former rectory. The condition of the volume is a signal that Gessner does not form a living part of the vigorous culture in which Heinrich finds himself in his uncle's village, but Heinrich nevertheless seizes upon him as a prophet.[53] When he returns to the city at the end of

---

[51]Keller decribes the uncle's house, which was once the "Landsitz eines Herren," later a "Pfarrhaus," as a combination of "das junkerhafte und das bäuerliche," *Der Grüne Heinrich*, III, p. 213.

[52]*Der Grüne Heinrich*, III, p. 118. We note also that the "theater," which cultivates illusion, and actors, who live in a separate subculture on the periphery of society, were symbols, particularly in *Wilhelm Meister*, but also in *Nachsommer*, of the dangers that lie in wait for the *Bildungsroman* hero.

[53]*Der Grüne Heinrich*, III, p. 224. Keller makes it clear that at this point Heinrich is especially in need of some corrective influence: „Überall, wo ich blätterte, war von Natur, Landschaft, Wald und Flur die Rede; . . . ich sah meine Neigung hier den Gegenstand eines großen, schönen und ehrwürdigen Buches bilden, ... Ich liebte sogleich diesen Mann und machte ihn zu meinem Propheten. . . . Es ist bei der besten Erziehung nicht zu verhüten, daß dieser folgenreiche und gefährliche Augenblick nicht über empfängliche junge Häupter komme, unbemerkt von aller Umgebung." (III, p. 225)

the summer to begin his apprenticeship with Habersaat, Heinrich continues in his unhealthy line of development, for Habersaat's art school/workshop is a sort of anti-*Bildungsroman* castle which shelters the young hero from the salutary contact with Swiss society.[54] The harm that has been done by the year with Habersaat is obvious when Heinrich returns to the country the following summer. Having once seen through both the technical limitations and the lack of any genuine pedagogical interest on the part of his mentor, Heinrich was forced to fall back on his own resources. He let his imagination run free and took great pleasure in pawning off fantastic figures and imaginary landscapes as *Studien* from the immediate vicinity.[55] When Heinrich shows some of the same paintings to his uncle as examples of his artistry, the honest man, though no critic, quickly spots the flaw, and calls his nephew up short with the observation: „Diese Baume . . . sehen ja einer dem andern ähnlich und alle zusammen gar keinem wirklichen."[56] The

---

[54]Keller dismisses any claim that Habersaat might seem to have for our respect with the following remark, *Der Grüne Heinrich*, IV, p. 54: „. . . so begriff er vollständig das Wesen heutiger Industrie, deren Erzeugnisse umso wertvoller und begehrenswerter zu sein scheinen für die Käufer, je mehr schlau entwendetes Kinderleben darin aufgegangen ist." As a type, Habersaat is familiar to us from the pages of Dickens. We might note here that there is a Dickensian element toward the end of Keller's *Bildungsroman*, in the unforeseen inheritance from the old *Trödelhändler* in the "Kunststadt," (Munich).

[55] See *Der Grüne Heinrich*, IV, p. 67: „So erfand ich . . . noch viel wunderlichere Menschen, zerlumpte Kerle, die ich dem Refektorium zutrug, um ein tüchtiges Gelächter einzuheimsen. Es war ein nichtsnutziges und verrücktes Geschlecht, welches eine Welt bildete, die nur in meinem Gehirne vorhanden war, . . . "

[56]*Der Grüne Heinrich*, IV, p. 70: Heinrich immediately recognizes the validity of the criticism: „Ich stand beschämt da als ein Mensch, der voll närrischer und eitler Dinge ist, und die mitgebrachte *künstliche Krankheit*

uncle's criticism of Heinrich's work is identical in essence with that made much later by the sophisticated Lys, who accuses Heinrich of being a „spiritualist," that is, one who takes his themes and subjects from his own head, instead of from the world.[57]

The influence the uncle exerts on Heinrich is greatly augmented by influences from the community at large. This community becomes completely visible during one of Heinrich's later visits to the country, on the day of the *Wilhelm Tell* performance. In his work for the *Tell* festival Heinrich first discovers his real love for Switzerland and his true vocation as an active contributor to the community life and spirit. During the midday banquet on the day of the performance Heinrich hears his (and Keller's) views on Swiss citizenship articulated by the *Statthalter*, who places the altercation between the innkeeper (who played the part of Tell) and the lumber merchant in its proper perspective. Heinrich had been upset by the innkeeper's energetic defense of his personal advantage, a behavior which Heinrich felt was out of character for the popular hero.[58] The *Statthalter* reminds him that only men such

---

verkroch sich vor der einfachen *Gesundheit dieses Hauses* und der ländlichen Luft" (Emphasis added).

[57]*Der Grüne Heinrich*, V, 175-76: „Wir haben also einen Spiritualisten vor uns, einen, der die Welt aus dem Nichts hervorbringt! . . . Sie wollen sich nicht auf die Natur, sondern allein auf den Geist verlassen, weil der Geist Wunder tut und nicht arbeitet!"

[58] *Der Grüne Heinrich*, IV, 189-90: „Die Unterredung hatte einen peinlichen Eindruck auf mich gemacht; besonders am Wirt verletzte mich dies unverhohlene Verfechten des eigenen Vorteils, an diesem Tage und in so bedeutungsvollem Gewande; solche Privatansprüche an ein öffentliches Werk, von vorleuchtenden Männern mit Heftigkeit unter sich behauptet, das Hervorkehren des persönlichen Verdienstes und Ansehens widersprachen durchaus dem Bilde, welches von dem unparteiischen Wesen des Staates in mir lebte und das ich mir auch von den berühmten Volksmännern gemacht hatte."

as the innkeeper and the lumber merchant, who are willing and able to keep their own house secure and in order, can be of real service to the community in times of need.[59] The *Statthalter*, of course, is merely formulating the lesson of the *Bildungsroman* first learned by Agathon—that a man concerned with the reforming of society and social institutions, such as Tell, must be concerned also with personal survival.[60] The innkeeper and the lumber merchant are exemplary figures who represent Keller's idealized Swiss citizenry. That Heinrich is almost ready to embrace this ideal before he leaves on his ill-advised mission to Germany is symbolized most exquisitely by his visit late that same night with Judith, for Judith—more than his uncle, more than the innkeeper or the lumber merchant, more than anyone else in the entire novel—symbolizes the health, the goodness, the naturalness and the vitality of rural Swiss society, and she, more than anyone else, represents the (for Heinrich still) seemingly mutually exclusive concerns with personal survival and social reform.[61]

---

[59]*Der Grüne Heinrich*, IV, 191.

[60] Personal survival is not very difficult in *Der Grüne Heinrich*. Heinrich experiences the problem in its most fundamental form when his money runs out in Germany, but his predicament is clearly the result of his own neglect. As soon as he rolls up his sleeves and goes to work he finds society quite willing to meet him halfway. In contrast with the earlier *Bildungsromane*, personal survival emerges as a problem only in isolation from society.

[61]Ten years later, of course, Heinrich has learned to appreciate fully this remarkable woman. He relates how she used the money she won in a lottery to help found a new community in the New World, how her good sense and energy were important factors in the success of that community, but also, how she was quick to protect her interests against the dangers from the lazy and unscrupulous elements in the new settlement. He concludes by noting, *Der Grüne Heinrich*, VI, p. 316: „der *Selbsterhaltungstrieb* war mit einer großen *Opferfähigkeit* so glücklich in

That Heinrich is not able to comprehend this natural harmony until after his disillusioning experiences in Munich is due partly to the fact that the corrective influences of the healthy Swiss society began to work on him in force only after his firm decision to become an artist. But Heinrich's ability to benefit fully from the experience of rural Swiss society was further compromised by his relationship to Anna and her father. This old schoolmaster's criticism of the *Statthalter's* views on citizenship, a criticism which is directed more at the character of the man than the substance of his remarks, tends to support Heinrich's earlier belief that it is unworthy of a man to allow personal interest to come before the interest of the community.[62] Heinrich is inclined to reject the schoolmaster's criticism, for he notes, „Daß für alles dies rüstige Volk die Freiheit erst ein Gut war, wenn es sich seines Brotes versichert hatte,"[63] but a remark about the difficulty of finding one's true work or calling in life, which was included in the schoolmaster's criticism, had touched Heinrich to the quick and prevents his coming to a decision.[64]

Heinrich's relationship to the schoolmaster and his daughter Anna presents perhaps the most problematical segment of the novel. On the one hand, for example, the schoolmaster's criticism of the Statthalter is not substantiated by later developments in the novel. Heinrich learns in Munich not only that he must work for a

---

ihr gemischt, daß sie die Leute und mit ihnen sich selbst . . . über Wasser hielt, . . ." (Emphasis added).

[62] The schoolmaster says, for example, *Der Grüne Heinrich*, IV, p. 194: „Er [der Statthalter] hat nicht den Mut, auf einen Tag brotlos zu werden; . . . wie gesagt, er hat ein dunkles Grauen vor dem, was man Brotlosigkeit nennt."

[63] *Der Grüne Heinrich*, IV, p. 197.

[64] *Der Grüne Heinrich*, IV, p. 197.

living—the schoolmaster had never disputed that[65]—but also, as the *Statthalter* had maintained, that he must be ready to defend vigorously his own rights and his own advantage. He gains the respect and the friendship of Schmalhöfer—another foster-father figure—by steadfastly insisting on the agreed rate of payment for the flagstaffs, even though his energy and industry will bring him more money than the old man had originally anticipated paying him.[66] On the other hand, however, the schoolmaster's remarks probe some of the darker corners of Swiss democracy, and his criticism of the *Statthalter* does not seem completely out of character for the thoughtful public servant, Keller. Similarly, while Heinrich's youthful relationship to Anna adds a problematic, even tragic dimension to his personality, the painful separation from her must be regarded as a victory over an unhealthy aspect of his personality.

Heinrich's relationship to Anna has been oversimplified in this analysis in order to show it in the perspective of the problem at hand. Heinrich's mistaken idea that he is to become a painter is, as we have seen, a direct result of his isolation from society, of his excessive (albeit externally caused) preoccupation with himself. When Heinrich visits his uncle in the country he re-establishes an essential contact with society. But then, when he takes the familiar path over the mountain to the home of the schoolmaster, he regresses into isolation from this society. The schoolmaster lives in a typical *Biedermeier* retreat from the world.[67] After the death of

---

[65] *Der Grüne Heinrich*, IV, p. 197, the schoolmaster says: „Wer essen will, der soll auch arbeiten."
[66] *Der Grüne Heinrich*, VI, p. 85: It is the first time that Heinrich can say: "Ich fühlte mich hier ganz auf einem sicheren Grunde."
[67] See *Deutsche Vierteljahrsschrift für Literaturwissenschaft und Geistesgeschichte*, ed. Paul Kluckhon and Erich Rohacker (Halle/Saale: Max Niemeyer Verlag, Volume XIII. The whole first quarter fascicle of

his wife he had relinquished his official position in society as village schoolmaster in order to devote himself to his books and to cultivate his garden. He is, Keller tells us, the exact opposite of the uncle, who turned his back on his urban background—"urban" by rural Swiss standards—and on his earlier clerical training to devote himself completely to the land and the rural community life. The schoolmaster has succeeded so well in overcoming his peasant background that now his only approach to nature is through his books.[68] Anna, who has grown up in this "unhealthy" seclusion from the community, is almost pure spirit when compared with her

---

Volume XIII, pp. 1-206, is devoted to the phenomenon „Biedermeier." Paul Kluckhon's article, „Biedermeier als literarische Epochenbezeichnung," pp. 1-43, begins the series. On page 36 Kluckhon writes: „Nur der Schweiz durfte man vielleicht eine Sonderstellung zugestehen, die ihrer besondern politischen Situation und deren Einfluß auf die Menschen entsprechen würde. Eine biedermeierliche Lebensführung und Dichtung, abgetrennt vom Politischen, von der Gemeinschaft der Eidgenossenschaft, des Kantons, der Stadt, der Gemeinde würde dem Wesen des Schweizer Bürgers zuwiderlaufen."

[68] The description of the contrasts between the two men is worth citing in full, *Der Grüne Heinrich*, III, p. 233: „Dort wohnte auf einem einsamen und abgelegenen Hofe ein Bruder meiner Tante mit einer jungen Tochter, . . . Ihr Vater war fruher Dorfschulmeister gewesen, hatte aber nach dem Tode seiner Frau sich in jenen beschaulichen Waldhof zurückgezogen, da er ein hinlängliches Vermögen besaß, und gerade das Gegenteil meines Oheims darstellte. Während dieser von städtischer Abkunft und in einigen geistlichen Studien aufgewachsen, dieses alles hinter sich geworfen und vergesse hatte, um sich ganz der braunen Ackererde und dem wilden Forste hinzugeben, strebte jener, von bäurischem Herkommen und bescheidener Bildung, allein nach milden und feinen Sitten, auch dem Leben und Ruhme eines Weisen und Gerechten und vertiefte sich in beschauliche, geistliche und philosophische Spekulationen, betrachtete die Natur nach Anleitung einiger Bücher, und freute sich, vernünftige Gespräche anzuknüpfen, . . . „

flesh-and-blood cousins across the mountain. She is a sickly *Schöne Seele*, and, like the *Schöne Seele* of the *Lehrjahre*, is incapable of playing an active role in social life.[69]

When Heinrich first visits the country he feels more at home—apart from the shyness which characterizes his behavior toward Anna—in the seclusion of the schoolmaster's house than with his uncle in the village. He is more at ease with his bookish friend than amid the rough and tumble of his cousins and their suitors. But already during the second summer Heinrich notices a change in his relationship to Anna's father, a change that in large measure derives from his growing experience of the real, material world.[70] It is naturally more difficult for him to distance himself in the same way from Anna, to whom he is bound by young love. He is also confused by his awakening sexual drives, and by his religio-culturally conditioned tendency to divide the world into a realm of the spirit and a realm of the flesh. Lys, we remember, accused Heinrich of being a "spiritualist," and Heinrich himself, in his taking leave of Judith, refers to the "besseren Teil meiner selbst,"[71] by which, of course, he means his spiritual side. But such a dualistic conception of man and of the universe runs counter to Keller's

---

[69] There seems to be a literary reference to the *Schöne Seele* of the *Lehrjahre* in Katherine's recounting of Anna's severe childhood illness, from which she *apparently* fully recovered, *Der Grüne Heinrich*, V, p. 35: We should not forget that, according to our analysis, Natalie's aunt was a warning for Wilhelm Meister against too much seclusion, against too much "spirituality."

[70] See, for example, *Der Grüne Heinrich*, V, p. 36: „Der Schulmeister nahm ein Buch, die Nachfolge Christi von Thomas a Kempis . . . Aber ich hatte durch den letzten Sommer die Lust an solchen Erörterungen fast gänzlich verloren, mein Blick war auf sinnliche Erscheinung und Gestalt gerichtet, . . . "

[71] *Der Grüne Heinrich*, V, p. 90.

realism and to the monism of his mature Weltanschauung. [72] Heinrich begins to sense the inevitability of a break in his delicate relationship with Anna long before he can understand the necessity of the break.

The process of Heinrich's education may be considered a gradual, sometimes painful wrenching loose from and overcoming of the isolation-bred spiritualism of his youth, a spiritualism of which Anna is the most delicate and alluring embodiment. A decisive turning point in his development comes during the *Tell*-festival, for which Heinrich has spent weeks and months in preparation, but which turns out quite different from what he had anticipated. We know from the earlier portions of his story that Heinrich had always enjoyed such public celebrations, and, as he noted, such an undertaking as the performance of *Wilhelm Tell* was too much in the spirit of his father for his mother to object to his participation. [73] But Heinrich does not participate in the festival quite in the spirit of his father, for he—innocently, to be sure—attempts to exploit this celebration for his own, quite personal ends. He intended to use the celebration to lure Anna out of her isolation into the real world, but what happens is that Anna retreats into even more profound isolation, and Heinrich is caught in his own trap. [74] As soon as the young "philosopher" explains to Anna that everyone expects her to play a real part in the celebration she becomes panic-stricken and starts for home. Heinrich rides after her, so that she will not be without an escort, and when, almost accidentally, they do assume their roles as Bertha von Bruneck, that is when Anna, for an instant, symbolically participates in the community *Tell*-festival, when she is confronted

---

[72] See Reichert, *Basic Concepts*, p. 125.

[73] *Der Grüne Heinrich*, IV, p. 161.

[74] Heinrich refers, *Der Grüne Heinrich* (IV, p. 200) to the „Schlinge, . . . welche ich ihr so harmlos gelegt."

with the real world across the mountain from her sheltered home, the world of flesh and blood and sexual drives, her essential nature is violated, and she receives a shock from which she does not recover. She returns home to begin the final stages of her complete spiritualization, which is death. But Heinrich returns to the communal celebration, and, later that night, amid the rain- and wind-swept fruit trees of her garden, life, in the person of Judith, bares her elemental power and irresistible charms to the confused but awakening youth.

It is, of course, impossible within this limited discussion to examine all the various influences at work in the various stages of Heinrich's development away from the subjective, romantic spiritualism symbolized by his attraction to Anna, to the whole-hearted endorsement of life, with all its fullness of joy and tragedy, symbolized by his reconciliation with Judith in the wonderful concluding chapter, "Der Tisch Gottes." What is most important is the now-clear fact that the distinctions mentioned much earlier, in Chapter 2, between the *Bildungsroman* hero's two modes of world encounter—through direct personal experience and through a mentor's interpretation—have lost much of their validity in Keller's, *Der Grüne Heinrich*, and with the blurring of these distinctions the traditional *Bildungsroman* castle has ceased to occupy a prominent position in the development of the hero. Society is not regarded as a malignant force against which the hero must be protected. On the contrary, as indicated by several *anti-castles*—Habersaat's art school and, to a lesser extent, the schoolmaster's retreat—continuous contact with society is regarded as essential for the healthy development of the individual.

On the other hand, the theory that Switzerland is itself a castle, a sheltering enclave within the larger community of Germany and Europe, should not be interpreted too literally. It is certainly true that Heinrich's experiences in Switzerland tend to be of the positive kind, that Heinrich is cultivated and nurtured in a healthy way by these experiences, and that his experiences in Germany tend to be more or less negative experiences, which lead to a kind of picaresque *déniaisement* or disillusionment. But the differences are really more of degree than of substance. To be sure, Heinrich is handled a bit more roughly in Germany; he is buffeted a bit more by life in the big city, but German society also has plenty of positive experiences to offer him, such as his discovery of the German university and, in the person of Hulda, of the German working class. On the whole, we must conclude, Keller's faith in the essential goodness and perfectibility of man, though it may be founded in his positive experience of Swiss society, is too profound to permit him to view contemporary German society with a pessimism equal to that of Stifter, or Immermann, or even Goethe before them.

A factor which tends to militate against a positive interpretation of Heinrich's experiences in Germany is the presence there of a seemingly traditional *Bildungsroman* castle. Heinrich is visibly broken, at the end of his rope, in full retreat, when he stumbles upon the castle of the *Graf*. Heinrich is apparently in the same untenable position as Agathon before he is offered sanctuary by Archytas, or as Wilhelm, before he discovers the Society of the Tower. The analogy can be extended by noting that the *Graf*—though, in this case, unknowingly—had already helped Heinrich by his purchase of the landscapes from Schmalhöfer, much as Archytas had worked behind the scenes to free Agathon from the jail in Syracuse, and much as the *Turmgesellschaft*, acting in secret, had stepped in at critical points to aid Wilhelm. But the analogy is weakened, except for purposes of contrast, by the fact that Heinrich's desperate state cannot be regarded as a result of a threat from society—it is merely the result of a purely personal dilemma. The analogy is further weakened by the fact that the *Graf*'s castle, if it can be considered a *Bildungsroman* castle at all, cannot be compared with the castles in *Wilhelm Meister* and *Nachsommer*. There is perhaps a certain validity in comparing the *Graf*'s castle with Archytas', for the *Graf*, like Archytas, does offer asylum to representatives of progressive, enlightened views; but since one of these men, Peter Gilgus, is a complete fool, [75] and since there is little evidence in the novel that these men are really in need of asylum because of their views, this aspect of the *Graf*'s castle may be discounted. The traditional *Bildungsroman* castle, especially in *Wilhelm Meister* and *Nachsommer*, serves to protect something of intrinsic value which is endangered by the storm of events, and the typical inhabitant of such a castle is looking for a "son" or an heir to whom he can pass on his treasures, his cultural tradition. The *Graf*, to be sure, is something of an art collector, and he too expresses the wish that he had a son, but it would nevertheless be wrong to view his castle as a cultural repository in the tradition of *Wilhelm Meister* and *Nachsommer*. He is tired of the weight of tradition, he tells Heinrich as they inspect the dusty family archives.[76] If he had a son, he says, he would sell his whole estate and move to the New World, „um in der verjüngenden Volksflut unterzutauchen."[77]

If the *Graf*'s castle were indeed a *Bildungsroman* castle in the tradition of the *Oheim*'s castle in *Wilhelm Meister* and Risach's *Rosenhaus* in *Nachsommer*, Heinrich would have acceded to the

---

[75] Peter Gilgus, who enters the picture just after Heinrich had been "converted" to the teachings of Feuerbach, should not be regarded as a satire on the philosopher, for the Graf is a warm supporter of Feuerbach, but as a satire on Feuerbach's naïve supporters, who expect the teachings of their hero to transform the world.

[76] *Der Grüne Heinrich*, VI, 197. The Graf uses the word „adelmüde," analogous to the "europamüde" popular in the 1830s and '40s.

[77] *Der Grüne Heinrich*, VI, 198.

*Graf*s' insistence that he remain, and have eventually discovered Dortchen's feeling for him. He would have married her, just as Wilhelm Meister and Heinrich Drendorf married their respective Natalies in their respective *Bildungsroman* castles. But Heinrich is anxious to return to Switzerland, and the *Graf* himself must applaud his decision not to stay.[78] In Switzerland, to which he returns at the time of a great populist movement, he will begin to prepare himself for a life of public service, and in Switzerland he will eventually be reunited and reconciled, symbolically through the person of Judith, to his society and to his time.

We can underline further the differences between Keller's Swiss *Bildungsroman* and the true or German *Bildungsroman* by examining one more example of the absence of a castle in Keller's novel in a situation where one might be expected. The lumber merchant, we remember, is an exemplary figure, a representative of a healthy element in Swiss society. We read of him that „Er . . . stimmte in den politischen Fragen *im Sinne des Fortschrittes*, aber ohne viel Umstände, indem er mehr durch sein Beispiel als durch Reden wirkte."[79] Archytas, Natalie and Lothario, and Risach, all were able to effect changes (*wirken*) through the power of example (*Beispiel*), but in each case their ability to effect changes was contingent on their being, in the sense of personal entelechy, on a being which is not possible except in a certain isolation from society—hence the need for the sometimes quite elaborate protective castles. But the lumber merchant's ability to effect

---

[78] See *Der Grüne Heinrich*, VI, pp. 282-83: „Ich hatte den sonst so ruhigen Mann nie so aufgeregt gesehen; die bloße Vorstellung, daß ich unmittelbar in eine Republik gehe und mich an deren öffentlichem Leben beteiligen werde, schien ihm andere verwandte Vorstellungen und alte Leiden der Unzufriedenheit zu erwecken."
[79]*Der Grüne Heinrich*, IV, 183: (Emphasis added).

changes through the power of example is not contingent on such factors. His is an example not of being, but of becoming, of action:

> . . . Er wollte die Sache der Freiheit und Aufklärung nach der Weise eines klugen Fabrikanten betrieben wissen, welcher nicht darauf ausgeht, mit ungeheuren Kosten auf ein Mal ein kolossales Prachtgebäude herzustellen, in welchem er die Arbeiter zur Not beschäftigen konnte, sondern der es vorzieht, unscheinbare räucherige Gebäude, Werkstatt an Werkstatt, Schuppen an Schuppen zu reihen, wie es Bedürfnis und Gewinn erlauben, bald provisorisch, bald solid, nach und nach, aber immer rascher mit der Zeit, daß es raucht und dampft, pocht und hämmert an allen Ecken, während jeder Beschäftigte in dem lustigen Wirrsal seinen Griff und Tritt kennt . . . Sein Wohnhaus lag mehr wie eine Arbeiterhütte, als wie Herrenhaus dazwischen hingeworfen, . . . [80]

The lumber merchant, in a German novel of the period, could have easily appeared as a representative of the destructive forces of modern society which threaten traditional values.[81] But Keller makes this figure into a symbol of his optimistic faith in the essential goodness and perfectibility of society, and a spokesman for his belief that all real progress is part of a deep organic change that is brought about by the daily commitment of individuals at all levels and stations of life. Keller minimizes the importance of the conservative—in the sense of *erhaltenden*—forces in the struggle for social progress, and with them, the importance of an intellectual or cultural elite. The *Graf* belongs to such an elite, but he knows that he is powerless to effect the type of changes in

---

[80] *Der Grüne Heinrich*, IV, pp. 183-85.
[81] In Droste-Hülshoff's *Biedermeier* novella, *Die Judenbuche*, and in Freytag's *Soll und Haben*, for example, the *Holzhändler* and *Holzdiebe* fulfill such a symbolic role.

German society that are occurring organically in Switzerland. He is aware that the intellectual revolution has, at least temporarily, far out-distanced the social revolution in Germany—a condition which, as we argued in Chapter 2, is largely responsible for the development of the *Bildungsroman* in Germany—but he is not particularly disturbed by this awareness.[82] He is, in the end, not much more than an interested spectator in the drama of change that he sees being acted out on the stage of Europe.

The near quietism that characterizes the *Graf*'s ultimate relationship to his time contains the vigorous germ of pessimism that Keller was able to isolate and contain with the help of the essentially healthy Swiss body politic. One of the chief sources of pessimism in the nineteenth century must be regarded as the growing awareness of the relative helplessness of the enlightened individual in the face of cataclysmic social upheavals, a dilemma for which the German *Bildungsroman* offers the pratico-moral solution of a retreat to a castle and an effective working within narrowly defined lines. Keller, while he must acknowledge the practical insignificance of any given individual, is able still in *Der Grüne Heinrich* to circumvent the seemingly necessary pessimism by positioning for "enlightenment" a broader social base. It is said of Heinrich's father, for example, the he shared „Das offene und treuherzige Hoffen der guten Mittelklasse auf eine bessere, schönere Zeit der Wirklichkeit, ohne von den geistigen Überlieferungen . . . etwas zu wissen,"[83] and the *Graf* says of Dortchen,

---

[82] Heinrich says of him, *Der Grüne Heinrich*, IV, pp. 212-13: „Der Graf gehörte geistig und zum Teil auch persönlich dem Verbande von Männern an, welche den begeisterten Kultus des Philosophen forderten, wenn er auch nicht die Ansicht und die Hoffnung teilte, daß er zunächst die politische Freiheit unfehlbar bringen müsse."

[83] *Der Grüne Heinrich*, III, p. 11.

„daß sie ganz auf eigene Faust nicht an Unsterblichkeit glaubt,"[84] in other words that she achieved her progressive ideas quite naturally, without the help of books and long years of study, or even much contact with artistic or cultural traditions.

In the tragic figure of Römer—one of the artist figures about whom we must say a few words before concluding the discussion of *Der Grüne Heinrich*—Keller compresses the despair of the artistic and intellectual elitist who had hoped to change and direct society from above and from without. Römer is a kind of *Bildungsroman* hero gone wrong, one who has failed to learn the lesson of personal survival. Within the context of Keller's *Bildungsroman* Römer is an example and a warning for Heinrich of the dangers that await the individual who isolates himself from society and still believes that he alone holds the key to society's ills.[85] It is symptomatic of Römer's failure that he cultivates his appearance, even at the cost of undermining his health,[86] because the type of influence that he can exert on society, like the influence exerted by Archytas, Natalie, Lothario and Risach, is contingent on his *being*, or at least *seeming to be*, more than his contemporaries. It is a mistaken idea, which,

---

[84] *Der Grüne Heinrich*, VI, p. 202

[85] *Der Grüne Heinrich*, V, p. 50: „. . . darauf deutete er mir an, daß alle Fäden der europäischen Politik in seiner Hand zusammenliefen und daß ein Tag, eine Stunde des Nachlassens in seiner angestrengten Geistesarbeit, die seinen Körper aufzureiben drohe, sich alsobald durch eine allgemeine Verwirrung der öffentlichen Angelegenheiten bemerklich mache . . ." and, II, p. 44, „Freilich, wäre er zu seinem Recht und zu seiner Freiheit gekommen, so würde im selben Augenblick die Mäusewirtschaft aufgehört haben und ein freies, lichtes und glückliches Zeitalter angebrochen sein."

[86] See *Der Grüne Heinrich*, V, p. 54: „Ich erfuhr erst später, daß Römer, während unsers Verkehrs fast immer gehungert und dabei seine spärlichen Mittel beinahe nur für den Unterhalt einer sauberen äußeren Erscheinung geopfert hatte."

like Heinrich's bragging and squandering during his *Lügenzeit*, is partly a result of and partly a contributing factor to his relative isolation within society.[87]

It is characteristic of Keller's melioristic *Weltanschauung* that he does not allow the pessimistic megalomania of the tragic artist—a figure so dear to nineteenth- and twentieth-century literature—to undermine his belief in progress and the perfectibility of human society. He does not allow any doubts regarding the ability of the gifted man, the artist or the intellectual, single-handedly to right the wrongs and cure the ills of the present to cloud his vision of an organically evolving, progressive Swiss society. Römer, who is unable to conceive of social progress that is not dependent for direction and guidance on his genius, ends his career as a social reformer in an insane asylum. In his own way, he is a "spiritualist," one who had placed too much faith in the power of his own mind, and too little in the natural genius of the people.

The remark by Lys—besides Römer the only true artist figure among Heinrich's acquaintances—about spiritualists, miracles, and idleness[88] touches the heart of Keller's *Der Grüne Heinrich* and lends support to our interpretation of Römer's failure and the significance of this failure for Heinrich Lee. But this remark also provides a slightly different perspective for viewing the difference between Keller's Swiss novel and the German *Bildungsroman*. Agathon's hope—that he could change the heart and the ways of

---

[87] On his way home from Munich, after frightening the forester away from the old woman by means of the skull of Albertus Zwiehan, Heinrich reaches the conclusion, „daß das Fundament all des anmaßlich brutalen Gebauschens eine grenzlose Eitelkeit sei," *Der Grüne Heinrich*, VI, p. 149, and he asks himself—a latter-day St. Augustine—VI, p. 151, „aber warum soll man sich denn von ihnen unterscheiden, sich über sie erheben? Um auf dieses Erhobensein selbst wieder eitel zu werden?"

[88] See note 57 above.

the tyrant by means of his own example and counsel—was in essence a hope for a miracle, as was Wilhelm Meister's dream of changing German society through the agency of the stage. Both Agathon and Wilhelm learn to live with a good measure of disillusionment, but, in fact, neither is forced to give up his belief in "miracles," which is nothing more than the belief in the power of the spirit to have a direct effect in the real, material world. As repeatedly noted, Archytas and the exemplary figures in the *Lehrjahre* and in *Nachsommer* all are able to effect change (*wirken*) more by virtue of what they are than by what they do.[89] In contrast, all the exemplary figures—not just the lumber merchant—in *Der Grüne Heinrich* are important for Heinrich less by virtue of what they are than by virtue of what they do. All of them—his uncle, the innkeeper, the lumber merchant, Schmalhöfer, Lys, and Erikson, including even the journeyman carpenter who made Anna's coffin, Hulda, and, of course, Judith—all have essentially the same admonition for Heinrich that he give up his childish belief in miracles, roll up his sleeves, and work toward the fulfillment of the miracle about which he dreams, which, of course, is the miracle of a transformed society.[90] The *Graf*, who is himself not so much an exemplary figure as a formal counselor to Heinrich, gives him the

---

[89] We note here that the important verb *wirken*, for which an exact English equivalent does not exist, is the one used in German versions of the New Testament to refer to Christ's "working" or "performing" of miracles. The English word "perform" vaguely suggests that the miracle is more the result of what the "performer" is (or seems to be) than of what he actually does.

[90] It is easy to forget, perhaps, that this is the essence of Heinrich's *Heimatsträume*. Heinrich, of course, is not able to interpret his dream until later, but then he actually does refer to himself as a *Weltverbesserer*, *Der Grüne Heinrich*, VI, p. 300: „So besaß ich kein Recht, unter diesem Volke mitwirken zu wollen, nach dem Worte: Wer die Welt will verbessern helfen, kehre erst vor seiner Türe."

same advice. When Heinrich remarks that he wishes to study a few years before devoting himself to the service of his country the *Graf* advises him to skip the formal study—the cultivation of his spirit or intellect—as his sole occupation and begin work immediately:

> . . . wie die Dinge einmal stehen, würde ich mit besonderen Studien keine Zeit mehr verlieren, . . . An deiner Stelle würde ich mich ruhig erst ein wenig umsehen und dann, nötigenfalls als Freiwilliger, ein unteres Amt übernehmen und schwimmen lernen, indem du sofort ins Wasser springst. Machst du es zur Regel, jeden Tag daneben einige Stunden staatswissenschaftliche Sachen zu lesen und zu überdenken, so bist du in wenig Zeit ein praktischer und hinlänglich gebildeter Amtmann zugleich.[91]

The important distinction between Keller's advice for his *Bildungsroman* hero and the advice given by the writers of German *Bildungsromane*—Wieland, Goethe, and Stifter—may be summarized by a simple analogy. These writers, directly or indirectly under the influence of German idealism, believe that society will be transformed by means of the spirit, much in the way that Christ, at the marriage feast of Cana, transformed water into wine by an act of his will and by virtue of his entelechy as the Son of Man. While Keller's contemporaries began to lose faith in the power of spirit to effect such a transformation, Keller called their attention to a new source of faith. While we may not transform water into wine by a direct act of our will, Keller seems to say, we may yet bring about the miraculous transformation naturally, by working with nature, learning as we go, planting, cultivating, harvesting, and pressing the grape.

The analogy is a simplistic one, and therefore potentially misleading, but it does, I believe, point to an essential difference between Keller's novel and the other novels more strictly in the German tradition, a difference which is reflected in the absence of

---

[91] *Der Grüne Heinrich*, II, 443.

a real *Bildungsroman* castle in *Der Grüne Heinrich*. Such castles are, in the last analysis, citadels of the spirit, whether, as in the case of *Agathon*, they merely provide a place of quiet and refuge for study and contemplation, or, as in the case of *Wilhelm Meister* and *Nachsommer*, they, in their function as "cultural vaults," serve to preserve, in art objects, the physical expressions of "spirit." Keller argues that this way—the way of even comparative isolation of an elite and a too-anxious concern with the preservation of spirit from contamination in the material world—lies not fruitfulness, but madness. Each of the three German novels we have examined ends with the hero secure in his castle. Heinrich Lee, in contrast, still has no permanent residence when Judith returns from America. The final scenes of the novel, the scenes of Heinrich's reconciliation to Judith and to life, take place in the open or in a public inn—underlining their lack of isolation, the immediacy of their contact with the ingredients for the working of the modern miracles, with fellow men and with nature.

CHAPTER 6: WORLD LITERATURE AND THE GERMAN TRADITION

With the publication of Thomas Mann's *Buddenbrooks* early in the twentieth century the German novel made its first convincing bid since Goethe's *Wilhelm Meister* for recognition as an equal among the great novels of Spain, England, France and Russia. Kafka and Hesse soon added their masterpieces, to give the German novel a presence in world literature that it had lacked during the previous centuries. It remains, of course, to be seen, whether *Die Buddenbrooks* and *Der Zauberberg*, *Der Prozeß* and *Das Schloß*, *Der Steppenwolf* and *Das Glasperlenspiel* will be able to maintain their position beside *Don Quixote*, *Tom Jones*, *Tristram Shandy*, *Les Misérables*, *War and Peace*, and *Crime and Punishment*. The very fact, however, that the twentieth-century German novel is being translated, read, and studied abroad, whereas the German novels of the eighteenth and nineteenth centuries are hardly read or even known outside of German-speaking areas, suggests that at least some of the works of Thomas Mann, Franz Kafka, and Hermann Hesse have earned a lasting place in world literature.

The question that we will pose and partially answer in this concluding chapter is the following: To what extent does acquaintance with the *Bildungsromane* of the previous centuries increase the understanding and appreciation of the novels of Mann, Kafka, and Hesse? In other words, to what extent are the well-known twentieth-century German novels part of a definable but lesser-known German tradition? In seeking to answer this question we shall attempt, first, to summarize our findings from the preceding five chapters concerning the German *Bildungs-roman*, and then to relate Mann's *Zauberberg* and Hesse's

Glassperlenspiel to this tradition. It should be re-emphasized here that no effort can be made to do full justice to these novels. The thesis remains essentially what it was in Chapter 1, namely that the six novels therein selected are "peculiarly German,"[1] that they belong to a peculiarly German tradition, and that any thoroughgoing discussion of these novels should begin with an awareness, at least, of the assumptions, the direction, and the thrust of this tradition.

Survey of the German *Bildungsroman*: A Summary

The rise of the *Bildungsroman* in late eighteenth-century Germany is closely connected with German social and intellectual history. The first *Bildungsroman* hero, Wieland's Agathon, may be regarded as a descendent of the moral heroes of the seventeenth-century courtly novel. Because Wieland was an adherent of eighteenth-century Enlightenment views, moral action for Agathon involves a commitment to humanity and to social progress. Because Wieland's experiences of German society corresponded roughly to the experience which had brought forth the picaresque novel in the countries to the west generations earlier, Agathon, the moral hero, is afforded a picaresque experience of society. Wieland's concern to preserve his and his hero's intellectually conditioned social commitment despite his disillusioning experiences of society—an essentially extra-literary consideration, as we noted—resulted in the prototype of the *Bildungsroman*. The

---

[1] See Mann's own *Vorwort*, „Für Studenten der Universität Princeton," *Der Zauberberg*, I, p. xvii: „In der Tat ist der ‚Zauberberg' ein sehr deutsches Buch, er ist es in dem Grade, daß fremdländische Beurteiler seine Weltmöglichkeit vollkommen unterschätzen."

solution to the dilemma, which involves practical as well as moral considerations—the reconciliation of the morally driven social reformer to the seemingly incorrigible society—is effected by the hero's retreat, not to an island, which would be a retreat from his moral duty, but to a castle, which becomes a symbol of his peculiarly ambivalent relationship to his society.

In Goethe's *Wilhelm Meister* the question that lies at the heart of the *Bildungsroman*, the question concerning the relationship of the morally committed social reformer to a delinquent world, is elucidated in specifically contemporary terms. The contemporary dimension of the problem corresponds to a worsening of the dilemma for the reformer; whereas in the statically conceived society of the "classical" world Agathon had experienced a threat to his personality—only as a result of an over-zealous, too ambitious attempt at changing the world, Wilhelm Meister began to experience such a threat in his own parental home. According to Goethe, contemporary, dynamic society, in changing, is in the process of destroying or losing the very things that are prerequisite for the development of a full and true moral personality as well as for organic social evolution. The castles in Goethe's *Bildungsroman* consequently have a conservative function that goes beyond the asylum function of Archytas' villa.

Even more than *Wilhelm Meister*, Stifter's *Nachsommer* emphasizes the need for conservation, or restoration, „re-creation." Both Goethe and Stifter have given their novels roughly contemporary settings to show the need for protecting not only the person of the hero but also a cultural tradition and way of life considered essential to the healthy development of that person and of society. The *Oheim*'s castle in *Wilhelm Meister* and Risach's *Rosenhaus* are both situated in rural environments. Wieland, who had not given his novel a contemporary setting, was still able to set up his hero at the end of his wandering in a rather open "castle" in an urban setting. In other words, with Goethe's introduction of contemporary terms in the *Bildungsroman*, there is an obvious shift in the direction of greater isolation from society, a shift which becomes more obvious in Stifter's *Nachsommer*—even to the extent that the balance between contact with and isolation from society that the *Bildungsroman* castle supposedly symbolizes becomes precarious and somewhat theoretical.

Keller, in contrast to Goethe and Stifter, approved of the changes taking place in contemporary society, or did so when he first wrote *Der Grüne Heinrich*. In his *Bildungsroman* the idea that the conservation of a cultural tradition in isolation from the storm winds of the present is necessary for ultimate progress, for organic, positive change, is not so much criticized as rejected out of hand. For the individual, too great isolation from society leads to the imbalance or warping of personality which Keller calls "spiritual-ization." In other words, Keller's *Der Grüne Heinrich* offers a reverse image of the *Bildungsroman*.

In using Keller's Swiss *Bildungsroman* as a reference point from which to view the novels more strictly within the German tradition, we may arrive at the following conclusions as to the direction and thrust of the tradition as it continues into the twentieth century: From Goethe's *Wilhelm Meister* on, the *Bildungsroman* hero must not only discover the proper balance between contact with and isolation from society, he must also learn to temper his desire to serve the betterment of society with a judicious amount of will to preserve the achievements and human values of the past. In *Nachsommer* as compared to *Wilhelm Meister*—that is, with the passing of time—the will to preservation necessitates increased isolation from contemporary society, a fact which compromises more radically the hero's ability to have a direct influence in society and which exposes him to the danger of "spiritualization" in Keller's sense of inability to live or function normally in social life. The following sections propound that these two important moments in the German *Bildungsroman*—the suspension of the moral hero in the *Spannungsfeld* between the will to serve the changing society and the will to preserve a cultural heritage, and the increasing tendency toward preservation at the expense of an effective role in society—lie at the heart of the great *Bildungsromane* of the twentieth century.

An Approach to *Der Zauberberg*

The more superficial similarities between *Zauberberg* and the other five novels taken as the basis for the investigation of the *Bildungsroman* were already noted in Chapter 1. Hans Castorp is an orphan figure who leaves his society in the "flatlands," encounters several foster-father figures in the "castle," Berghof, before returning, "reconciled," to serve his society quite modestly as a foot soldier in World War I. Before we direct our attention to the fact that the "castle" which he visits does not resemble the proto-type of the *Bildungsroman* castles of the *Lehrjahre* and *Nachsommer*, we must consider a striking resemblance between this novel and Goethe's classical *Bildungsroman*. We are referring to Wilhelm's relationship with his grandfather and his grand-father's art collection.

Sandwiched in between the report of Hans' arrival and the description of his first full day at the sanatorium is a leisurely flashback giving some of the particulars of the young hero's family and background in Hamburg. The elder Castorp, after the death of his wife, a none-too-successful or diligent merchant, left Hans an orphan in possession of a moderate fortune at the age of seven years. The chapter which elaborates on his life between the death of his father and his arrival in Switzerland bears the rather curious but telling title: "Von der Taufschale und vom Großvater in zwiefacher Gestalt." [2] It soon becomes obvious that Hans' grandfather, like Wilhelm Meister's, is a representative of a tradition and a way of life that is threatened with destruction by the powerful economic forces governing Hamburg's bourgeois elite. As in *Wilhelm Meister*, the young hero's sojourn in his grandfather's house was for him a time of excitement, mystery, and expanding horizons. The comment, therefore, that „Zu seinem Schaden geschah es nicht" [3] when he moved out of his grandfather's house to the house of his *Oheim*,[4] must be understood ironically.

The section of Chapter 2 which tells of Hans' life with Konsul Tienappel bears the equally ironic title „Bei Tienappels. Und von Hans Castorps sittlichem Befinden." During his brief stay with his grandfather, Hans had begun to gain an appreciation of a type of *Sittlichkeit* that is founded on a profound sensing of one's participation in a tradition that transcends the individual and the momentary. The *Taufschale* with the inscribed names of seven generations of Castorps had been Hans' key to an experience of life as something greater than that of an individual, to a continuum between the living and those who have lived. These experiences with his grandfather provided the seed for his philosophical speculations on the nature of time, which concern Hans during

---

[2] *Der Zauberberg*, Chapter 2, p. 26

[3] *Der Zauberberg*, I, p. 40.

[4] Konsul Tienappel is actually an uncle of Heinrich's mother. See *Zauberberg*, I, p. 41. The picture that emerges is one of external correctness and polish, but internal hollowness and lack of human warmth. Mann notes, for example, that Hans' guardian, despite the family ties, does not fail to deduct his quarterly two percent for the management of the orphan Hans' inheritance. The Tienappel residence, for all its stately splendor, situated in a garden, „in dem auch nicht das kleinste Unkraut geduldet wurde," resembles in its sterile „emptiness" Wilhelm Meister's parental home.

most of his stay at the sanatorium. His childlike analysis of his grandfather into everyday grandfather and the grandfather in his *wahrer Gestalt*, as "representation," as he appeared in his portrait, in full, traditional ceremonial regalia, is an indication of the boy's intuitive understanding of a deep existential basis for *Sittlichkeit*. Hans' *sittliches Befinden* in the home of his guardian Tienappel is a caricature of what might have been his had he been able to grow up under the influence of his venerable grandfather.[5] When he emerges from Tienappel's tutelage, Hans is a polished, *sittlicher* drone, a hypersensitive, directionless automaton of meaningless habits and passionless desires. Judging from the imaginative, almost philosophical inquisitiveness of the seven-year-old in his grandfather's house, and the awakening of a similar drive in the man during his stay on the *Zauberberg*, it is reasonable to assume that Hans' stay in the hermetic isolation of the Tienappel residence is responsible for his bloodless and spiritless condition at the beginning of the novel.

In the sanatorium Hans begins to experience the world as it had apparently ceased to exist for him when he moved in with his mother's uncle. It is a world of mystery and fascination for Hans, peopled in part, according to his early, vague impressions, by members of some spiritual or intellectual elite. As Hans gradually becomes *akklimatisiert* to this world, he begins to view the life of the bourgeoisie of Hamburg, in the flatlands below, with an increasingly critical eye. He begins to expand his intellectual and spiritual horizons beyond the perimeters of *Ocean Steamships*—a

---

[5] The figure of the grandfather, of course, is not completely free of caricature. On the whole, however, he is perhaps the most positively described of all the characters in the novel, none of whom escape some sort of caricature. He is as venerable in his old age as he was strong in his prime, „eine scher zu fällende, im Leben zäh wurzelnde Natur," *Der Zauberberg*, I, p. 27.

symbol of the narrow, utilitarian basis of his education up to his arrival at the sanatorium—through his association with the foster-father figures Settembrini, Naphta, and Behrens, and through independent study, observation, and exploration. There is, then, some basis for comparing the Berghof with the more traditional *Bildungsroman* castles in *Agathon, Wilhelm Meister* and *Nachsommer*. Compared with the sterility and "emptiness" of the Tienappel milieu, the *Berghof* is a place where the hero may experience and profit from the cultural heritage and intellectual cross-currents of early twentieth-century Europe.

But in many ways the *Berghof* seems to be the exact opposite of a *Bildungsroman* castle. Rather than offering Hans a measure of isolation from the larger society, the sanatorium seems to be a microcosm of Europe, torn by the same powerful forces that were—beneath the surface, perhaps—rending the fabric of pre-World War I European society. Instead of being a realm of light and order as are the earlier *Bildungsroman* castles, the sanatorium offers a panorama of an irrational world of passion, death, decay, hope, and despair. In comparison with the world of the *Berghof*, the home of Hans' uncle in Hamburg might seem more like the sheltering *Bildungsroman* castle.

That neither the Tienappel residence nor the sanatorium fits into the pattern of the *Bildungsroman* castle that emerges in the novels of Wieland, Goethe and Stifter points to a questionableness in the designation *Bildungsroman* for Mann's *Zauberberg*.[6] The relationship of these two pseudo-*Bildungsroman* castles to the castles in the *Bildungsromane* of Wieland, Goethe, and Stifter—and hence, the relationship of Mann's novel to the German *Bildungsroman*—will become clearer if we examine the

---

[6] Thomas Mann himself referred to this novel as a parody of the Goethean *Bildungsroman*. See Köhn, p. 473.

relationship of Hans to the most important of the foster-father figures in *Zauberberg*, to Settembrini.

Hans had just begun to distance himself from the *flatlands* and to explore the association of sickness with a higher form of life when he met Settembrini. Hans' new acquaintance startles him with the vehemence of his rejection of the idea that sickness is somehow *vornehm*. [7] Though Hans is first amused by the appearance of the Italian, who reminds him of an organ grinder, Settembrini's remarks make an impression on him, and, as the friendship between the two men evolves toward a true father-son relationship—replete with the skepticism of the "son" toward the ideas and assumptions of the "father"—these remarks serve as a reminder to him and to the reader that despite the shallowness and narrowness of the bourgeois life Hans left in Hamburg, there is something about this life that is sadly missing in the morbidly self-centered society of the *Berghof*. This something is, of course, a superficial kind of health, and the concomitant ability for concern with questions of broader social significance than the purely personal and immediate ones of the patients at the *Berghof*. That the society in the flatlands is making little or no real progress in

---

[7] See *Der Zauberberg*, I, p. 143: „Erlauben Sie mir aber, Ihnen zu bemerken, daß ich Ihren Deduktionen nicht folgen kann, da ich sie ablehne, ja ihnen in wirklicher Feindseligkeit gegenüberstehe." And p. 144: „Nun denn, nein! Krankheit ist durchaus nicht vornehm, durchaus nicht ehrwürdig—diese Auffassung ist selbst Krankheit oder sie führt dazu. . . . Vernunft und Aufklärung . . . haben diese Schatten vertrieben, welche auf der Seele der Menschheit lagerten, —noch nicht völlig, sie liegen noch heute im Kampfe mit ihnen; dieser Kampf aber heißt Arbeit, mein Herr, irdische Arbeit, Arbeit für die Erde, für die Ihre und die Interessen der Menschheit, und täglich aufs neue gestählt in solchem Kampfe, werden jene Mächte den Menschen vollends befreien und ihn auf den Wegen des Fortschrittes und der Zivilisation einem immer helleren, milderen und reineren Lichte entgegenleiten."

solving the pressing social problems of the day, Settembrini, much in the tradition of the *Bildungsroman*, would attribute to its failure to look to the enlightened humanist, such as himself, for instruction and leadership. Settembrini's arguments have only little appeal for Hans, however, largely because of the fact that the Italian, no less than Tienappel, fails in his thinking and life to confront the dominant aspect of reality so visible to Hans after his arrival at *Berghof*, namely irrationalism, the existence of dark, elemental, irrational forces and desires.

Settembrini is a representative of that tradition of a belief in progress which begins in the German novel with Wieland's *Agathon*. He is also a member of that tradition of liberal radicalism which led to the series of revolutions in nineteenth-century Europe. His grandfather, as he fondly relates, was a *Carbonero*, a member of the group of revolutionary republicans who worked toward the dismantling of the old order in Italy during the nineteenth century. Since Hans' grandfather[8] was a representative of an older, nobler, conservative element in the German bourgeoisie, reminiscent of the grandfather and *Oheim* figures in *Wilhelm Meister*, the stage is set, it would seems, for a struggle and a compromise between the *Sittlichkeit* of treasured institutions and the morality of social reform such as we find in the *Bildungsromane* of Goethe and Stifter. It is, however, part of the problematic nature of Hans' predicament that there is no real conflict between the conservative moment represented by Hans's grandfather and the radical moment represented by Settembrini. Both men talk in terms and think in concepts that seem to have lost their validity against the backdrop of the fathomless irrationalism of the present.

---

[8] We read of the old Castorp that he „hatte auf . . . alte Institutionen weit mehr gehalten als auf halsbrecherische Hafenerweiterungen und gottlose Großstadt-Alfanzereien, hatte gebremst und abgewiegelt, wo er nur konnte." *Der Zauberberg*, I, p. 33.

Settembrini speaks to Hans over a gulf that is just as impassable as the one that separates him from the world of his grandfather. Settembrini and Hans' grandfather are united in the singular inapplicability of their dreams of human dignity to the experience of the present. Settembrini's talk of light and reason is of little help to Hans, who has just experienced irrationalism first-hand in his darkling relationship to Clawdia Chauchat. There is no road back, and if there is any road at all to the vision of humanity born in the past, it leads—as the dream on the mountain seems to con-firm—relentlessly on through the irrationalism of the present.[9]

The inadequacy of foster-father figure Settembrini, both with regard to advice and to example, for the needs of orphan figure Hans is underlined on the one hand by the fact that he does not possess a castle of his own—aside from his very modest lodgings in the village of the sanatorium—in which he might create the world of light and reason about which he dreams, and, on the other—assuming with Keller that a castle is not at all called for—by the fact that he is not able to leave the isolation of the *Zauberberg* and work among the people in the *flatlands*. The absence of a true *Bildungsroman* castle in *Zauberberg*, of course, provides a sort of formal corroboration for the assertion that Mann's novel is a parody of the German *Bildungsroman*. The word parody, however, does not convey the depth and the genuineness of the concern with which Mann treats the themes of the traditional *Bildungs-roman* in *Zauberberg*. As the above paragraphs suggest, there is little doubt that in this novel Mann makes a concerted effort to deal positively with the questions that are the subject matter for the

---

[9] Clear indications of this plight are the absence of any true *Bildungsroman* castle and the fact that for Hans there is no return home to his grandfather's house, not even symbolically as in *Wilhelm Meister*, only a departure for the war-torn land where his grandfather's house had been.

Bildungsroman—the stifling sterility of the bourgeois order of the day, the need for a broad cultural base for the development of the full moral and social personality, and the dangers which precisely contemporary society holds for the developing personality. His novel may be regarded as an attempt to restate and reaffirm the importance and the immediacy of the questions treated in the German *Bildungsroman*, questions which are made more pressing than ever by the fact that the traditional answers no longer seem applicable. The criticism of the German tradition in Keller's *Bildungsroman* is confirmed and broadened in *Zauberberg* to include the Swiss novel itself. Keller's optimistic vision of humanity—founded, as we noted, on his experience of the liberal institutions of Swiss society, and represented, to a certain extent here by Settembrini—is unconvincing when viewed in the context of another and later Swiss institution, the sanatorium at Davos. But the *Berghof* is not the whole world, and must itself be viewed in the broader context of the *flatlands*. Neither the shallow, rational world of Tienappel (dominated almost completely by economic considerations, but committed superficially to social goals) nor the profoundly irrational world of the *Berghof* (dominated by the reality of sickness, death, and committed almost wholly to the pursuit of intensely personal ends) gives a complete picture of the real world. The hope is left open at the end of the novel that out of the symbolic merging of these two worlds in the festival of death that was World War I a new order of light and love will someday emerge.

Das Glasperlenspiel: Analysis of a Tradition

A reader of Hesse's *Glasperlenspiel*, perhaps the most important and lasting of all his major works, should be struck by the extent to which this novel represents a coming to terms with the problem complex that lies at the heart of the German *Bildungsroman*. The figure of Joseph Knecht is flanked on both sides by friends, Plinio and Tegularius, who illustrate, by their failings, the dimension of the *Bildungsroman* problem. Kastalien itself is a *Bildungsroman* castle replete with foster-father figures and with all the questionableness of that institution that came to light in Keller's *Der Grüne Heinrich*. The main character in the novel, Joseph Knecht himself, is a classical *Bildungsroman* hero, who tries to resolve his dilemma according to the formula first given in Wieland's *Agathon*, „im kleinen Kreise wirksam zu werden."

Kastalien, the name itself suggestive of a castle, is a „päd-agogische Provinz," somewhat like the one Felix is sent to in *Wilhelm Meisters Wanderjahre*. The setting of the novel is in the future, some several hundred years after the tumultuous „feuilletonistischen Zeitalter," and thus, to a certain extent, corresponds to the „Zeit der Abklärung" which Stifter felt would sooner or later follow the storm of the present, a time in which the practical necessity of cultivating the spirit and intellect and the cultural heritage of Europe would be generally acknowledged and thus supported by the state.[10] Kastalien is a world set apart from the larger society, to serve the larger society by virtue of what it can accomplish and become only in isolation from it. The suggestion that all is not right in Kastalien, however—that Kastalien is perhaps not serving society well enough to prevent a backsliding into the „feuilletonistische Zeitalter," that there may be dangers for society and for Kastalien in the too great distance of the province from society and in the too intensive cultivation of the spirit and of tradition—these ominous notes are sounded early by the young *outsider* in Kastalien, Plinio Designori.[11]

---

[10] See *Glasperlenspiel*, pp. 106-07, and p. 176.

[11] See *Glasperlenspiel*, p. 167: „Plinio, der sich in der Rolle des outsiders gefiel." It is part of Plinio's tragic role, of course, that he is an outsider

Plinio first appears as a self-confident man of the world whose commitment to anything beyond his own person is in question. But in the student debates between him and Knecht, debates which the officials recognized as of sufficient importance to make them an institution of the school, the future Magister Ludi gains his first insight into the problematic nature of Kastalien's very existence.[12] Plinio later appears as a tragic figure, a *Bildungsroman* hero who failed, one who has fallen victim to the classical mistake of the social reformer.[13]

The danger in Kastalien to which Plinio was the first to react becomes visible in the person of Tegularius, who is almost pure spirit, a *Schöne Seele* of sorts in this womanless world, a person completely incapable of surviving outside the sheltered confines of the institution. That Tegularius' sickliness is a direct result of his exclusive cultivation of the "spirit" is indicated by the fact that he is the most sophisticated if not the most perfect master of the game, that ultimate answer to the cultural vaults of Goethe and Stifter.[14] Knecht learns to regard his brilliant but unstable friend as a forerunner of a type of *Glasperlenspieler* and *Kastalier* that will become more common as Kastalien succumbs to the dangers implicit in the too-great cultivation of the spirit in isolation from the problems and concerns of the "real" world, the larger society.

Tegularius' complete isolation from the large society is further indicated by his inability to think of ordinary political history as a

---

not only with respect to the sheltered world of Kastalien, but with respect to the larger society as well.

[12] See *Glasperlenspiel*, p. 169.

[13] Namely, in his impatience with the elitism and isolation of Kastalien, Plinio underestimated the dangers which society holds for the morally driven social reformer. Plinio's experiences as a social reformer exactly parallel those of Agathon, who discovered one day to his horror that society had changed him more than he had changed society.

[14] See *Glasperlenspiel*, p. 198:

legitimate field for study.[15] Knecht first discovered the importance of such studies as a result of his friendship with Pater Jacobs, the Benedictine scholar at the monastery Marienfels. It was also a result of his association with this man that the Catholic Church, or at least the Benedictine order, became an exemplary symbol for Knecht. The Church has survived for some 2000 years, he thinks—though this is nowhere expressly stated—because of its ability to cultivate the spirit without losing contact with the flesh and blood, bread and wine of the real world. Knecht apparently concludes that such a feat cannot be duplicated by Kastalien. Knecht's "legendary" end, his slipping below the surface of the mountain lake, might be interpreted as his personal contribution to the returning of the spirit to the elemental world. There is also at least the suggestion of a hope that the youth left standing on the shore may be able to combine in his own person the worldliness of his father with the spiritualism of the great man from Kastalien. As he stands there tormented by the thought that he is partly responsible for the death of his teacher there comes over him the sense of a tremendous burden.

---

[15] Joseph Knecht tricks his friend into studying the history of the origin of Kastalien during the „feuilletonistisches Zeitalter" by requesting his help in the preparation of his petition to the authorities for permission to lay down his duties as Magister Ludi, but there is no indication that Tegularius actually profited by his historical studies. Knecht did not even consider telling his friend of his coming departure after the petition, as expected, was denied.

A LOOK BACK

As we look back now on the German *Bildungsroman* from the perspective of the last novel in our survey one important feature seems to distinguish the novels in the twentieth century from those of the eighteenth and nineteenth, and it is a feature which these novels share, to a certain extent, with Keller's Swiss *Bildungs-roman*. The twentieth-century novels, and Keller's nineteenth-century novel, are all, in a sense, open-ended. There is no "happy end" to these novels, as there was in the *Bildungsromane* of Wieland, Goethe, and Stifter, though there is a definite recon-ciliation and homecoming at the end of the second edition of *Der Grüne Heinrich*. But at the same time, true to the tradition of the *Bildungsroman*, there is no real tragedy and no despair at the end of these novels, all of which end on a strong upbeat of hope. Hope, as we noted, was the most important ingredient in the happy end of the traditional *Bildungsroman*. The main difference between the hope for a better world as expressed in the earlier *Bildungsromane* and those we examined in the twentieth century is that in the twentieth century the author of the *Bildungsroman* is unwilling or unable to cast his hope in the definite forms of the earlier *Bildungsromane*—and this corresponds, of course, to the absence of true *Bildungsroman* castles in the later novels. This unwillingness or inability on the part of the twentieth-century writers to state their hope in definite terms seems to correspond to a measure of disillusionment and uncertainty greater even than that which was characteristic, as we noted, of the author of the first *Bildungs-roman*. It may also, however, correspond to a profounder sense of hope, one which borders on religious faith, for the hope that is kept alive on the muddy battlefields of World War I and which rises with the sun over the scene of the death of Joseph Knecht is somehow less assailable than the hope that must be preserved in the carefully delineated confines of the traditional *Bildungsroman* castle.

WORKS CITED

Alewyn, Richard. „Erzählformen des deutschen Barocks." *Formkräfte der deutschen Dichtung*. Göttingen: Vandenhoeck & Ruprecht, 1963, pp. 21-34.

Alter, Robert. *Rogue's Progress: Studies in the Picaresque Novel*. Harvard Studies in Comparative Literature, No. 26. Cambridge, Mass.: Harvard University Press, 1964

Berger, Berta. *Der moderne deutsche Bildungsroman*. Sprache und Dichtung: Forschungen zur Sprach- und Literaturwissenschaft, No. 69, ed. Harry Mayne, Fritz Strich, and S. Singer. Bern-Leipzig: Paul Haupt, Akademische Buchhandlung, 1942.

Der Große Brockhaus. 16th ed. Wiesbaden: Eberhard Brockhaus Verlag, 1953-57.

Brunner, Horst. *Die poetische Insel: Inseln und Inselvorstellungen in der deutschen Literatur*. Germanistische Abhandlungen, No. 21. Stuttgart: J. B. Metzlersche Verlagsbuchhandlung, 1967.

Buddecke, Wolfram. *C. M. Wielands Entwicklungsbegriff und die Geschichte des Agathon*. Palaestra: Untersuchen aus der deutschen und englischem Philologie und Literaturgeschichte, No. 235. Göttingen: Vandenhoek & Ruprecht, 1966.

Dehn, Wilhelm. *Ding und Vernunft*. Bonn: H. Bouvier and Co., 1969.

Dilthey, Wilhelm. *Das Erlebnis und die Dichtung: Lessing, Goethe, Novalis, Hölderlin.* 7th ed. Leipzig and Berlin: Verlag B. G. Teubner, 1921.

Dobert, Eitel Wolf. *Karl Gutzkow und seine Zeit*. Bern and Munich: Francke Verlag, 1968.

Frenzel, Herbert A., and Elisabeth Frenzel. *Daten deutscher Dichtung*. 3rd ed. Cologne and Berlin: Kiepenheuer & Witsch, 1962.

Gay, Peter. *The Enlightenment: An Interpretation. The Rise of Modern Paganism*. 2 vols. New York: Alfred A. Knopf, 1967.

Gerhard, Melitta. *Der deutsche Entwicklungsroman bis zu Goethes ,Wilhelm Meister.'* Halle/Saale: Max Niemeyer Verlag, 1926.

Germer, Helmut. *The German Novel of Education 1792-1805: A Complete Bibliography and Analysis*. German Studies in America, No. 3, ed. Heinrich Meyer. Bern: Herbert Lang & Co., 1968.

Goethe, Johann Wolfgang von. *Werke*. Ed. Erich Trunz, 5th ed. 14 vols. Hamburg: Christian Wegner Verlag, 1962.

Greiner, Martin. *Die Entstehung der modernen Unterhaltungsliteratur: Studien zum Trivialroman des 18. Jahrhunderts*. Reinbek bei Hamburg: Rowohlt Taschenbuchverlag GmbH, 1964.

Hesse, Hermann. *Gesammelte Schriften*. 7 vols. Berlin: Suhrkamp Verlag, 1952.

Hoffmann, Werner. „Grimmelshausens ,Simplizissimus'—nicht doch ein Bildungsroman?" *Germanisch-Romanische Monatsschrift*, N. F. 17 (1967), 166-80.

Immermann, Karl Leberecht. *Werke*. Ed. Harry Mayne. 9 vols. Leipzig and Vienna: Bibliographisches Institut, [1906].

Jacobs, Jürgen. *Wielands Romane*. Bern: A. Francke Verlag, 1969.

Jost, François. "La Tradition du 'Bildungsroman.'" *Comparative Literature*, 21 (1969), 97-115.

Keller, Gottfried. *Sämtliche Werke*. Ed. Jonas Fränkel. 19 vols. Erlenbach-Zürich and Munich: Eugen Rentach Verlag, 1926-39.

Kluckhohn, Paul. „Biedermeier als literarische Epochenbezeichnung." *Deutsche Vierteljahrsschrift für Literaturwissenschaft und Geistesgeschichte*, 13 (1939), 1-43.

Köhn, Lothar. „Entwicklungs- und Bildungsroman: Ein Forschungsbericht." *Deutsche Vierteljahrsschrift*, 42 (1968), 427-73 and 590-632.

Korff, H. A. *Geist der Goethezeit*. 4 vols. Leipzig: Verlagsbuchhandlung von J. J. Weber, 1930.

Lammert, Eberhard. *Bauformen des Erzahlens*. Stuttgart: J. B. Metzlersche Verlagsbuchhandlung, 1955.

Lewis, R. W. *The Picaresque Saint*. Philadelphia and New York: J. B. Lippincott Co., 1959.

Lucács, Georg. *Werke*. 12 vols. Neuwied and Berlin: Hermann Luchterhand Verlag, 1964.

Mann, Thomas. *Gesamtausgabe der Werke*. Stockholm: Berman-Fischer Verlag, 1939.

Martini, Fritz. „Der Bildungsroman: Zur Geschichte der Theorie und des Wortes." *Deutsche Vierteljahrsschrift*, 35 (1961), 44-63.

McInnes, Edward. „Zwischen *Wilhelm Meister* und *Die Ritter von Geist*: Zur Auseinandersetzung zwischen Bildungsroman und Sozialroman im 19. Jahrhundert." *Deutsche Vierteljahrsschrift für Literaturwissenschaft und Geistesgeschichte*, 43 (1969), 487-514.

Mommsen, Wilhelm. *Die politischen Anschauungen Goethes*. Stuttgart: Deutsche Verlagsanstalt, 1948.

Ohl, Herbert. *Bild und Wirklichkeit: Studien zur Romankunst Raabes und Fontanes*. Heidelberg: Lothar Stiehm Verlag, 1968.

Pabst, Walter. „Literatur zur Theorie des Romans." *Deutsche Vierteljahrsschrift*: 34 (1960), 264-89.

Pascal, Roy. *The German Novel*. Toronto: University of Toronto Press, 1956.

Petsch, Robert. *Wesen und Formen der Erzählkunst*. *Deutsche Vierteljahrsschrift*: Buchreihe, No. 20. Halle/Saale: Max Niemeyer Verlag, 1934.

Reallexikon der deutschen Literaturgeschichte. Founded by Paul Merker and Wolfgang Stammler, 2nd ed. Ed. Werner Kohlschmidt and Wolfgang Muhr. 2 vols. Berlin: Walter de Gruyter & Co., 1955-64.

Reichert, Herbert W. *Basic Concepts in the Philosophy of Gottfried Keller*. University of North Carolina Studies in the Germanic Languages and Literatures, No. 1, Chapel Hill: The University of North Carolina Press, 1949.

Saine, Thomas P. "Wilhelm Meister's Homecoming." *Journal of English and Germanic Philosophy*, 70, No. 3 (1970), 450-69.

Schiller, Friedrich. *Briefe*. Ed. Fritz Jonas. 7 vols. Stuttgart: Deutsche Verlagsanstalt, 1895.

Schumann, Willy. „Wiederkehr der Schelme." *PMLA*, 81 (1966), 467-74.

Seidler, Herbert. „Wandlungen des deutschen Bildungsromans im 19. Jahrhundert." *Wirkendes Wort,* 11 (1961), 148-62.

Seidlin, Oskar. „Picaresque Elements in Thomas Mann's Work." *Essays in German and Comparative Literature*. University of North

Carolina Studies in Comparative Literature, No. 30. Chapel Hill, N. C.: University of North Carolina Press, 1961.

Sengle, Friedrich. *Christoph Martin Wieland*. Stuttgart: Metzlersche Verlagsbuchhandlung, 1949.

_____, "Der Romanbegriff in der ersten Hälfte des 19. Jahrhunderts." *Arbeiten zur deutschen Literatur 1750-1850*. Stuttgart: J. B. Metzlersche Verlagsbuchhandlung, 1965.

Shackleton, Robert. "French Literature: The 18th Century." *Encyclopaedia Britannica*, 1968.

Shaftesbury, Anthony Earl of. *Characteristics*. Ed. John M. Robertson. 2 vols. Gloucester, Mass.: Peter Smith, 1963.

Staiger, Emil. *Adalbert Stifter als Dichter der Ehrfurcht*. Heidelberg: Lothar Stiehm Verlag, 1967.

Stifter, Adalbert. *Der Nachsommer*. Ed. Max Stefl. 3 vols. Basel: Benno Schwabe & Co., 1954.

Viëtor, Karl. *Goethe*. Bern: A. Francke AG Verlag, 1949.

_____, „Probleme der literarischen Gattungsgeschichte." *Deutsche Vierteljahrsschrift*, 9 (1931), 425-47.

Wagner, Hans R. *Der englische Bildungsroman bis in die Zeit des ersten Weltkrieges*. Bern: A. Francke Verlag, 1951.

Wieland, Christoph Martin. *Ausgewählte Werke in drei Bänden*. Ed. Friedrich Beißner. Munich: Winkler Verlag, 1964.

Wiese, Benno von, ed. *Der deutsche Roman*. 2 vols. Düsseldorf: August Bagel Verlag, 1963.

Will, Wilfried van der. *Pikaro Heute: Metamorphose des Schelms bei Thomas Man, Döblin, Brecht, Grass*. Stuttgart: W. Kohlhammer Verlag, 1967.

Wilpert, Gero von. *Sachwörterbuch der Literatur*. 4th ed. Stuttgart: Alfred Kröner Verlag, 1964.

CURRICULUM VITAE[1]

On February 14, 1943, I, John Gadway, was born in Homestead, Florida, the second of six children and the only son of Mr. and Mrs. John Herbert Gadway. After completing my elementary schooling in Homestead, I graduated in June, 1961 from the South Dade High School. In September, 1961, I entered Tulane University on a full tuition, academic scholarship. In June, 1965 I received there a B.A. with a major in German, having spent my junior year at the University of Tübingen where I attended lectures by Professors Beißner, Ziegler, and Jens. In 1965 I was granted an NDEA Fellowship to continue as a graduate student in German at Tulane University. Between September, 1965 and June, 1969 I completed the coursework and the preliminary examinations for the PhD degree. Since September, 1969 I have been a full-time instructor at Southern Illinois University in Carbondale.

---

[1] As at time of submission to Tulane University, June, 1972.

APPENDIX: ABSTRACT TO THE 1972 DISSERTATION

THE CASTLE IN THE BILDUNGSROMAN

AN ABSTRACT

SUBMITTED ON THE TENTH DAY OF JULY, 1972

TO THE DEPARTMETN OF GERMANIC AND SLAVIC LANGUAGES

OF THE GRADUATE SCHOOL OF

TULANE UNIVERSITY

IN PARTIAL FULFILLMENT OF THE REQUIREMENTS

FOR THE DEGREE OF

DOCTOR OF PHILOSOPHY

BY

_____

(SIGNED)
JOHN F. GADWAY

APPROVED:

_____

(Signed)
Dr. Margaret Groban
(Chairman)

_____

(Signed)
Dr. Thomas C. Starnes
Dept. Chairman

_____

(Signed)
Dr. Ann R. Arthur

Although scholars generally agree that German's most important contribution to the European novel is the *Bildungsroman,* the agree less on which characteristics are fundamental to the form *Bildungsroman* and on which novels belong to this tradition. A consensus, however, establishes certain representative German novels as *Bildungsromane,* among them Wieland's *Agathon* and Goethe's *Wilhelm Meister* from the eighteenth century, Stifter's *Nachsommer* and Keller's *Der Grüne Heinrich* from the nineteenth, and Mann's *Zauberberg* and Hesse's *Glasperlenspiel* from the twentieth.

A preliminary examination of these six novels reveals a closer relationship between the Bildungsroman and the picaresque novel than is generally believed to exist. The Bildungsroman hero, like the picaroon, is an orphan or quasi-orphan who for much of the novel views society from the picaresque perspective of the outsider. Like the picaroon, he encounters one or more foster father figures who aid his orientation in the world. Distinct extra-artistic intentions on the part of the authors of picaresque novels and *Bildungsromane* account for the more striking differences between the picaroon and the genetically related hero of the *Bildungsroman.* The unproblematic roguery of the picaroon reflects the author's concern with social satire and exposé. The idealistic striving of the moral hero of the *Bildungsroman* reflects the author's concern with stating the relationship of the individual to a problematic society in positive terms. The concern of the foster father in the *Bildungsroman* with reconciling the moral hero to his imperfect society—a concern which contrasts sharply with the urbane cynicism of the foster father of the picaresque novel—reflects the German author's characteristic extra-artistic intentions.

The advice and the example offered by the foster father of the *Bildungsroman* is symbolized by the castle in which the hero typically finds him, for the residents of a castle, while sheltered to an extend from the dissipating forces of a society in a state of transition, may nevertheless—unlike the picaresque hero—have a social function as insiders in such a society. The body of this dissertation analyzes the changing nature and role of the "castles" and their exemplary inhabitants in the six *Bildungsromane,* providing a perspective on the evolution of the form.

The increasing importance and elaboration of the castles in *Wilhelm Meister* and *Nachsommer* parallel and increasing willingness on the part of the German novelists to shelter their developing heroes from the dissipating forces in society, even at the expense of their playing a direct role in the shaping of the evolving social institutions. Keller's *Der Grüne Heinrich*, which reverses the trend toward increasing isolation from society and increasingly elaborate protective castles, represents an implicit criticism of an idea central to the German tradition. For Keller, continuous contact with society, no isolation, is necessary for the development of the full, moral personality. In the twentieth century Keller's doubts concerning the value of the *Bildungsroman* castle are echoed in *Zauberberg* and *Glasperlenspiel*, but his optimism regarding the value of intimate social contact is tempered by the view, characteristic of the earlier *Bildungsromane*, that contemporary society poses serious threats to the survival of the moral personality.

AFTERWORD, 2013[1]

> *Du gleichst dem Geist, den du begreifst,*
> *Nicht mir.*

Faust

You may wonder what a dissertation on the German novel could possibly have to do with an attempt to find space within the modern scientific canon for ghosts, angels and free will. It turns out to be fairly obvious, once you notice it, but something I overlooked for a long time. If you'll turn with me now to examine a slice of German literary history, I'll show you how it fits in.

Quick, name a nineteenth-century German novelist whose work has stood the test of time. Think, in other words, of a nineteenth century German novelist you could place beside Mark Twain or Herman Melville in the United States; beside Charles Dickens or Thomas Hardy in England; beside Leo Tolstoy or Fyodor Dostoyevsky in Russia; or beside Émile Zola, Gustave Flaubert and others in France. You can probably add to the list from each country, and perhaps from other countries as well. I'll give you a minute to think or to consult the Internet.

OK, who do you have for Germany?

You can probably name a number of nineteenth century German philosophers of world stature, a few composers, a few scientists, perhaps even a mathematician or a politician. But where are the novelists? It's not like there was nothing going on in the German speech community of nineteenth century Europe, which

---

[1] Being Chapter 4 of *Here Be Angels: Sojourn in a Different World*, John Gadway, KanebeGone, September, 2013, ISBN-13: 978-0-9895710-0-5

included a large part of the Austro-Hungarian Empire, East Prussia, Liechtenstein, and part of Switzerland. This was the time when German became the language of science and German-language universities were among the best in the world. Based on a surging industrial and commercial sector, during this century Germany became the dominant power on the continent and began playing catch-up to the older imperial powers by colonizing parts of Africa and snapping up smaller properties in the Pacific. There was a tremendous balling up of cultural and political energy in nineteenth-century Germany that exploded in two world wars in the first half of the twentieth.

There was, in other words, plenty of raw material in this hundred-year span for novelists to work with. But nobody, it seems, was equal to the task. You cannot find a nineteenth-century German novelists to rank with the great American, British, French and Russian novelists of the time.

Why not?

The lack of world-class German novelists in the nineteenth-century is particularly puzzling when you consider their footprint in the previous and following centuries. A German novel published in 1774, Goethe's *Die Leiden des Jungen Werthers*, became the first bestselling novel in the modern sense.[2] It started a Europe-wide phenomenon known as "Werther Fever," which caused thousands of young men to dress in the blue-and-yellow waistcoats and breeches Werther was described as wearing in the novel, and more than a few young men to re-enact in real life the suicide with which the novel ends. Napoleon was so impressed with the book that he took a copy with him on his Egyptian campaign and even wrote his own sequel to it. Twenty-one years later, in the tumultuous

---

[2] Rousseau's *Émile* might be cited as an earlier counterexample, because of the enthusiasm with which it was received through Europe, except that it was a treatise, not a novel.

aftermath of the French Revolution, Goethe published his second novel, *Wilhelm Meisters Lehrjahre* (*Wilhelm Meister's Apprenticeship*), the prototypical *Bildungsroman*, or "novel of formation." It would be more than one hundred years before another German novel found a significant readership beyond the German cultural sphere. But then, in 1901, Thomas Mann burst upon the scene with Buddenbrooks,[3] followed by the breath-taking novel-fragments of Franz Kafka and Robert Musil, and the enthralling works by Alfred Döblin and Hermann Hesse.

What caused this sudden expression of literary talent? In my dissertation I argued that one could not appreciate these twentieth-century masterpieces without knowing the tradition in which these novelists were writing, a tradition virtually unknown outside the German-speaking community. Fortunately for me, my dissertation director at Tulane, Dr. Margaret Groben, agreed. Recently, while going through musty boxes containing my notes and marked-up drafts of my dissertation of forty years ago, I came across a letter from her dated March 14, 1971, commenting on Chapter 2 of my six-chapter dissertation. In the first paragraph she wrote the following:

> As I never before have had a first draft that did not seem to me to need considerable overhauling, I have, underneath my pleasure in your work, the uneasy feeling that it can't be true, that I cannot have read it carefully enough! . . . Your study gives me a new view of the *Bildungsroman* and invalidates my idea of why . . . [it] . . . is no longer possible in its pristine form.

While I was naturally pleased with this appraisal of my work, her letter marked the beginning of the end of my professional interest in the German novel and German literature in general. It

---

[3] For which he received the Nobel Prize in 1929.

became a struggle for me to stay focused on my dissertation. From the start I too had had "the uneasy feeling" that it could not be true; I had stumbled on something which, once stated, seemed obvious. Perhaps what I was at pains to explain was already well-understood by established literary historians. I searched the literature and wracked my brain: what was I missing? When Dr. Groben's remarks allowed me to accept the possibility that I wasn't missing anything, that I had noticed something that generations of scholars had overlooked, grandiose ambitions smoldering below the surface received a new supply of oxygen. I found myself eager to bring my now-recognized analytical ability and personal energy to bear on things of a more substantive nature than academic literary history.

Later I came to realize that my involvement with the German novel had been more consequential than I originally imagined. I also came to realize that in my dissertation I had not properly understood my own question. The more appropriate question was this: What had caused the German novel to virtually disappear from world literature for more than a hundred years? I think I have the answer now. The lack of world-class German-language novels in the nineteenth-century can be blamed on Goethe, who had charged *Wilhelm Meisters Lehrjahre* with a huge extra-literary moment that proved unwieldy in less masterful hands.

I will explain.

Goethe is Germany's Shakespeare, but also, in a real sense, her Benjamin Franklin and, to a lesser extent, her Lavoisier. With respect to his literary output, Goethe was by inclination a lyric poet and a dramatist, and only incidentally a novelist. But he was also a statesman, and, most importantly in his own estimation, a scientist. He was a polymath who got drawn into administrative duties on behalf of his patron, Karl August, Duke of Saxe-Weimar-Eisenach, although the political stage on which he operated was considerably smaller than Franklin's. He was a geologist who, at the time of his death, had the most extensive rock collection in Europe. He made significant contributions to anatomy, botany and morphology, an important field of scientific inquiry that he almost single-handedly created.[4] He was most proud, however, of his scientific magnum opus, *Zur Farbenlehre* (On the Theory of Colors), which he valued more than his entire literary output. In this work he follows meticulous observations on the perception of color with a direct attack on Newton's theory and his approach to science in general. He criticized the incomparable Newton for trying to reduce the perception of color—an intensely personal, subjective, psychological event grounded in physiology—to an impersonal, objective phenomenon, something "out there" that could be captured within mathematical equations.

Although Goethe's theory posed no real threat to Newtonian optics, many physicists, beginning with John Tyndall in the mid-nineteenth-century, and including later luminaries such as Hermann von Helmholtz in the late nineteenth and Werner Heisenberg in the early twentieth centuries, have commented on the acuteness of his observations and the fact that, if you accept his not-unreasonable assumptions, the analysis presented in the first part of *Zur Farbenlehre* explains the perception of color in a self-consistent way. [5] James Gleick reported that Mitchell Feigenbaum, the father of chaos theory, went so far as to say that Goethe had been right about color.

---

[4]It is because he stands at the headwater of this important branch of science that I compare Goethe, the scientist, with Lavoisier, the acknowledged father of modern chemistry. In *The Upright Ape: A New Origin of the Species*, (2007) Aaron G. Filler, provides an illuminating discussion of Goethe's poetic science.

[5] The second part of *Zur Farbenlehre* is devoted to a critique of Newtonian optics.

Goethe was a scientist from the old school who stayed close to the phenomena. It was fairly easy for the mathematically inspired classical physicists in the nineteenth century to find weaknesses in his theory of colors, but as twentieth-century physicists reinserted the observer at a critical juncture in the analysis of optical phenomena it became less easy to dismiss Goethe's criticism of the fundamental assumption behind Newtonian analysis.

Newton (and all classical physicists who followed him, up to and including Einstein) assumed that it was possible to comprehend the world objectively, that is, as something existing independently of any observations that could be made on it—the commonsense idea that the moon is there whether we observe it or not. Today theoretical physicists continue to dream of grasping ultimate reality in a completely objective mathematical model, often referred to as a "theory of everything," or TOE. For Goethe, a narrowly focused science that does not concern itself with man's intimate engagement with the world is destined to miss the most revealing features of the universe. In an often-quoted passage from *Zur Farbenlehre*, Goethe condemns the approach that seeks to ban the subjective component of observation:

> Man in himself, insofar as he uses his healthy senses, is the greatest and most accurate physical apparatus that there can be, and that is precisely what is of the greatest harm to modern physics, that one has, as it were, separated experiments from man and wants to know nature merely through what manmade instruments show, yes, wants to limit and prove thereby what nature can do.

One can only imagine what Goethe would have to say about today's string theorists, given the remoteness of their theorizing from the phenomena and their manifest lack of concern with the immediate experience of physical reality.

Goethe's great novel, *Wilhelm Meisters Lehrjahre*, is often mentioned in the same breath with Fielding's *The History of Tom Jones, a Foundling*, published in 1749—the year, coincidentally, of Goethe's birth. In fact, Fielding's novel cast a shadow in English literature comparable to Goethe's impact on the German novel. *Tom Jones* is frequently referred to as both a *Bildungsroman* and a picaresque novel. There are, in fact, clear aspects of both traditions in Fielding's novel, particularly with respect to the picaresque. Tom Jones, the foundling, is clearly an outsider to the genteel world into which an accident of birth inserted him, ideally positioned literarily to expose the foibles and the contradictions of contemporary society. And if you are not too particular with the definition of *Bildungsroman*, a term widely used synonymously with "novel of education," then the characterization stands: Tom Jones does indeed receive a moral education of sorts in the course of the novel, which allows him to reconcile his lusty, affectionate nature and impulsiveness with the demands of a necessarily flawed society. But "novel of education" is a far-too-loosely defined category to capture what is essential about the German tradition that began in earnest with Goethe's second novel. There is, in the German tradition, nothing comparable to the lightheartedness and comic relief that makes Fielding's novel readable even today, and which continued to characterize English novels until the later part of the nineteenth century. There is, in fact, an undercurrent of leaden seriousness in *Wilhelm Meisters Lehrjahre* that reflects Goethe's deep preoccupation with the forces unleashed by the French Revolution. It is helpful to think of his novel less as a stand-alone literary monument than as a direct appeal by a concerned scientist to his nation to discover a passage through the frightening social maelstrom that threatened to involve all of Europe. In Goethe's case, of course, the concerned scientist happened to be endowed with world-class literary gifts and unparalleled powers of observation.

What initially caught my attention about representative German novels from the late eighteenth to the mid-twentieth centuries was a structural feature that held true to form, from Christoph Martin Wieland's *Geschicte des Agathon* (*The History of Agathon*, 1776-1777)—the prototype of the form that Goethe perfected—to Mann's *Der Zauberberg* (*The Magic Mountain)* (1923-24), Kafka's *Das Schloß* (*The Castle*) (1926), and Hesse's *Das Glassperlenspiel* (*The Glass Bead Game*, usually translated as *Magister Ludi*) (1943). In each of these literary works, together spanning 170 years, a quasi-orphan figure encounters one or more foster-father-like mentors in a castle or a castle-like environment. In the nineteenth century these "castles," typified by Stifter's *Rosenhaus* (1857), had taken on a museum-like quality to which the hero could retreat for aesthetic and ethical orientation and some cultural R and R. By the twentieth century, with the possible exception of *Glassperlenspiel*, these "castles" had morphed into caricatures of what they had been for Goethe. In Mann's *Zauberberg*, Hans Castorp meets his mentors and his love interest in Berghof, a tuberculosis sanatorium in the Swiss Alps. The hero of Kafka's *The Castle* (begun in 1922), known simply as K., is never able to gain access to his would-be mentors, the mysterious authorities who govern the village surrounding the castle of the novel's title. In Hesse's 1943 novel, which is set perhaps 500 years in the future, the castle is a fictional Central European province, evocatively named *Castalia*, which has been set aside for the life of the mind, a place where music, art, mathematics and classical lang-uages could be cultivated for their own worth, without the intrusion of mundane concerns like politics or even technology.

In *Glassperlenspiel* there are many literary references to characters and places in Mann's *The Magic Mountain*, and the name of Hesse's main character's, Joseph Knecht, seems to be a clear reference to Joseph K., the hero of Kafka's 1925 novel fragment *Der Process* (*The Trial*), who encounters his own castle-caricature in the huge tenement building that houses the airless courtrooms where he is to be tried. But the overall thematic reference in Hesse's mature novel is clearly to Goethe's masterpiece. Like Goethe, who was writing *Wilhelm Meisters Lehrjahre* as the French Reign of Terror threatened to engulf the entire continent, Hesse, writing as the lights were going out in Nazi-dominated Europe; Hesse lived the urgency of preserving the cultural monuments and masterpieces of western civilization from the terrifying forces of Hitler's National Socialism. The entire province of Kastalien represents an imagined political institution-alization and idealization of the castles where Wilhelm encounters his mentors.

Hesse, like Goethe, saw the threat to civilization *not* from the brute force of armed mobs rioting in the streets, but, more insidiously, from a tendency observable in what he referred to in the novel as "the age of the feuilleton," a general drift toward materialism and superficiality. Like Goethe, he saw the present as a time when members of the new, technology-driven, powerful industrial class trivialized the cultural achievements of the past, which tended, historically, at least in Germany, to be cultivated by the old-money landed aristocracy. The threat, in Goethe's view, did not come from members of the underclass, who, in the final analysis, respond to good leadership. The threat to Western, essentially European, civilization came from a rising new-money class which assumed the power that comes with wealth without concern for the difficult-to-achieve foundation of a fully actualized moral personality.

Goethe's essentially conservative position, his rendition of an idealized landed aristocracy, is initially off-putting to modern sensibilities, particularly as it comes from a child of the Enlightenment, which emphasized universal education as a panacea for social ills; but his deep-seated concern with developments in contemporary society is understandable given the extremely disturbing events of the French Revolution. How do you explain a culture that produced scientists like Lavoisier and Laplace and philosophers like Diderot and d'Alembert descending so quickly in the aftermath of the French Revolution to the Reign of Terror, or the fact that the figure most associated with these horrors, Robespierre, was himself a child of the Enlightenment who, at one point, had argued for the abolition of the death penalty?

Hesse faced a similar question in his time: how could a madman like Hitler seize power in a society that had produced scientists like Boltzmann, Planck and Einstein, philosopher-scientists like Mach and Wittgenstein, and poets like Heine and Rilke? Hesse seemed to conclude that it was a kind of moral failure on the part of those best suited by intelligence and education for leadership to refuse to dirty their hands in the day-to-day business of public affairs. At the end of *Das Glassperlenspiel* Joseph Knecht leaves his prestigious position as "Master of the Game" in what he came to regard as the ivory tower of Kastalien to become the tutor of his childhood friend in the outside world, a person who had maintained contact with him during the years he was isolated from the larger society. Like Mann's Hans Castorp, who leaves the tuberculosis sanatorium in Switzerland to disappear in the battlefields of World War I, Knecht, who dies in a swimming accident just several days after taking up his tutorial responsibilities, fails to make a mark on the larger society to which he returns. As a generation of counter-culture American youth was to discover in the 1960s, Hesse was more interested in the kind of spiritual growth necessary to achieve the personal enlightenment that would allow one to escape the maya of the physical world.

In Goethe's *Bildungsroman*, Wilhelm abandons a secure position in his family's thriving commercial ventures to join a troupe of traveling actors. While living with this troupe he endures pretty much the same misadventures, temptations, affairs of the heart and trials that had traumatized both Fielding's *Tom Jones* and Samuel Richardson's *Clarissa* (1748); there is also much of the same tension between the rising bourgeoisie and the aristocracy that characterized the earlier English novels. Wilhelm is given many opportunities during the first three quarters of the novel to abandon his life with the traveling actors and return to a more conventional life as a merchant, but he perseveres in what, to the reader, is an increasingly quixotic venture. In a letter to his brother-in-law Werner, a wholesale merchant who represents the conventional career path open to Wilhelm, he explains, „ . . .mich selbst, ganz wie ich da bin, auszubilden, das war dunkel von Jugend auf mein Wunsch und meine Absicht." ("From my earliest days it has darkly been my wish and my intention to form myself, completely as I am.")

Wilhelm goes on to explain why his drive for what, after Maslow, we might call self-actualization is not possible within the confines of contemporary bourgeois existence.

> Ich habe nun einmal gerade zu jener harmonischen Ausbildung meiner Natur, die mir meine Geburt versagt, eine unwiderstehliche Neigung ... da ich aber nur ein Bürger bin, so muß ich einen eigenen Weg nehmen ... Nun leugne ich Dir nicht, daß mein Trieb täglich unüberwindlicher wird, eine öffentliche Person zu sein, und in einem weiteren Kreise zu gefallen und zu wirken.

> (I simply have an irresistible inclination toward that harmonious formation of my nature that my birth denies me . . . but since I am merely a Burgher [as opposed to a member of the nobility] I must make my own way. Now, I am not going to deny that my drive to

become a public person, to *work* (*wirken*) and find acceptance in a wider circle, becomes more insuperable each day.)

I emphasize the German word *wirken* and my translation with its English cognate "work" because of the special significance this word appears to have in Goethe's worldview. At one point Wilhelm complains bitterly that the bourgeoisie's ability to achieve anything in this world is limited to *schaffen* and *leisten*, which may be translated as "making" and "doing."[6]   In Wilhelm's usage these verbs suggest a sweaty pushing and shoving of objects external to oneself in a scramble to get ahead—a clear reference to the wholesale merchant's concern with material things, with things that are "out there"; Goethe's 1795 use of these words in this context may be read as a not-too subtle reference to his quite explicit 1794 criticism in *Zur Farbenlehre* of the physicists' obsession with objectively measurable quantities. *Wirken*, in contrast to *schaffen* and *leisten*, suggest the ability to have an effect by virtue of what a person *is* rather than what a person *does*. A person's ability to *wirken*, in other words, reflects what one has become as a result of personal striving, study, and self-actualization. There is, therefore, an inescapable whiff of magic in the concept—a mysterious kind of unmediated effect across space and time that so bothered Newton about his own theory of gravity. A man who is able to *wirken* is a man who is able to project the force of his will onto the course of history by virtue of the heft or gravity that his personality assumes as a result of his *Bildung*.

The realists among us may be tempted to dismiss Goethe's worldview as hopelessly romantic, and therefore unscientific. It would, in fact, be pointless to argue that his worldview was not informed by essentially romantic ideas, despite his well-known

---

[6] The German word 'schaffen' also means 'to create,' but that is not the sense in which it is used here.

rejection of romanticism as a literary movement in his maturity. But the question is not whether or to what extent Goethe incorporated romantic notions into his worldview, but rather—and this of far more general significance—whether having an essentially romantic or spiritual view of nature is ipso facto unscientific.

The extent to which a worldview is scientific in the broadest sense has less to do with preconceived notions of romanticism versus realism than with its ability to comprehend the world as it is, without prejudice. If the world is fundamentally mysterious—as it was for pre-scientific societies and, indeed, as it is increasingly revealed to be by science—then a worldview that mischaracterizes mystery as an artifact of ignorance ultimately to be dispelled by science is bound to miss the mark. The real question concerning the value of what Goethe referred to as his poetic science is the extent to which, by embracing *all* fact and *all* experience without prejudice, he maintained contact with reality. On that important issue the jury is in. By trusting his powers of observation and his own experience, Goethe was able to formulate hypotheses that have taken mainstream scientists two hundred years to validate. Today, appreciation for the depth of his scientific insights continues to grow.

Goethe had been fascinated by one of the seminal scientific events of his century—Lavoisier's demonstration that all matter could be reduced to repeating small elements, which we recognize today as chemical elements. He became convinced that the similarities among all multi-cellular life forms—plants and animals—reflected a common underlying elemental structure. His search for the archetypical plant—the *Urpflanze*—which he pursued during the early part of his *Italienische Reise (Italian Journey)*, was motivated by his observation that all parts of flowering plants are, in effect, modified leaves. This observation was soon recognized as an important contribution to botany. But

Goethe's later, more daring hypothesis—that the body plans of all animals, from arthropods to vertebrates, were also constructed on the basis of a similar repetition and modification of a basic modular unit—was met by derision. His younger contemporary, however, the great French biologist Étienne Geoffroy Saint-Hilaire, developed Goethe's idea further, arguing that the vertebrate body plan could be understood as a flipped and inverted version of the arthropod body plan, with the exoskeletons of insects, arachnids and crustaceans corresponding to the endoskeletons of the vertebrates, and the anus in one of the phyla corresponding, according to its embryological development, to the mouth of the other.

Only within the past few years has microbiological analysis of the function of the *Hox* gene complex established the cogency of the original insight obtained two hundred years ago on the basis of Goethe's careful observation of facts. Aaron Filler writes that the Hox complex "is the modern-day physical manifestation of the magnificent and lyrical idea that burst into [this] great poetic mind . . . [the] idea that all complex life—plant and animal—was assembled from modular units."[7] By employing what he described as "the greatest and most accurate physical apparatus that there can be," Goethe was able to connect the dots and see what it took reductionist biologists another two hundred years to appreciate.

Goethe was a scientist who also happened to be a world-class lyric poet, Germany's most famous dramatist, and, when the occasion demanded, a novelist. In his greatest drama Goethe described the prototypical scientist as an alchemist whose thirst for knowledge was matched by his hunger for life in general: Faust was driven to pursue esoteric knowledge by the same passion that drove him to pursue carnal knowledge of Gretchen. His first novel, *Die Leiden des Jungen Werthers*—which, in 1774, had taken Europe

---

[7] Aaron G. Filler, *The Upright Ape* (2007) pp. 43-44.

by storm—was the young Goethe's incautious baring of his passion to the world. Thirty-four years later he offered the world his mature vision of passion's ability to override a man's sense of self-preservation. The young Werther had committed suicide because he could not obtain the object of his desire; in a pact with the devil, the mature Faust surrendered his immortal soul in exchange for satisfying his passion in this world—preeminently a passion for knowledge and understanding. Goethe, of course, was neither Werther nor Faust, but when it came to passion, he knew whereof he wrote.

It is helpful to pause here to recall what it means to be passionate, which is just the opposite of what may come to mind when we hear the word. We tend to think of a passionate person as someone who takes vigorous action to further his or her cause or desire. For example, we might think of someone who mounts a passionate defense of liberty or of their honor. In other words, we tend to think of a passionate person as the initiator of action. But when we are passionate, the world is acting on us, we are more the object of the action, rather than the subject; we are suffering. Recall, for example, the passion of Christ. This distinction between the actor and the receiver of the action is reflected in the grammatical analysis of language. *The batter hit the ball out of the park.* That's the active voice. The subject of the sentence is the actor. *The ball was hit out of the park.* That's the passive voice. The subject of the sentence is the ball; it's being acted upon.

In passion, we are gripped by the world in a way that mocks the dream of comprehending reality objectively in mathematical formulae. In passion, we are the ball, not the batter. We may be flying, but not of our own volition. We have been moved. But if you were to model the event of the ball encountering the bat and flying out of the park mathematically, by objectifying the happening you would lose perspective and all sense of drama. The differential equations in which the laws of physics are expressed and which inform the model are known mathematically as unitary operators; they have an inverse, much like multiplication is the inverse of division. Models constructed on the basis of such operators can be run backwards just as well as forwards. From the perspective of the mathematical model of the event, the ball flying in from center field propels the bat to the shoulder of the batter to the same extent that the swung bat propels the ball over the fence. The batter, as agent—so important to the narrative from our naïve point of view—completely disappears in the mathematical model. There is no distinction between active and passive voice in the model because there is no voice at all, no agency and no object of passion.

It was because Goethe was intimate with the power of passion to move men to action that he was so pointed in his criticism of Newton. Goethe saw Newton as cold and austere, completely given to a belief in the power of reason to capture reality objectively in a mathematical formula, a powerful but icy intellect insulated from the weaknesses and vagaries of the flesh by his incomparable genius. This, indeed, is the picture one would get from reading Newton's published works. It is the image Newton tacitly endorsed and which was nurtured in the eighteenth century. What Goethe did not know, and what he could not have known, is that Newton's public persona, particularly as it was burnished in the eighteenth century by his enthusiastic followers, was a carefully cultivated construct that masked a far more complicated and conflicted relationship to reality. Today, historians of science understand that Newton was driven by the same hunger for esoteric knowledge that tormented Goethe's legendary Faust.

In the last decade of his life the great British economist, John Maynard Keynes, spent considerable energy and personal treasure to secure for Trinity College at Cambridge a then-recently rediscovered trove of Newton's unpublished writings that the physicist had carefully sequestered in a large trunk upon leaving Cambridge and entering his post-academic life as a public administrator. In an essay he had hoped to deliver to the Royal Society on the 300th anniversary of Newton's birth (1942), Keynes described the import of these unpublished works, which comprise perhaps a million carefully redacted words in Newton's meticulous hand. World War II prevented the event from being celebrated on the actual date of the tercentenary—Christmas day, 1942—and Keynes died several months before the celebration was rescheduled for the summer of 1946. But the essay, which Keynes' brother read to the Royal Society in the summer after the War, should be required reading for any student of physics, as well as for any scientist interested in the sociology of knowledge. Keynes, based on his study of Newton's own writing, made a convincing case that the incomparable physicist—who, during his most productive years at Cambridge, remained committed to esoteric studies—could be considered the last of the magicians dating back to Babylonia. I came away from my reading of this essay with the conviction that the greatest of physicists—well known to be hypersensitive to criticism and reluctant to publish anything that he could not prove mathematically—is in large measure responsible for the readiness of the lesser minds who followed him to dismiss any hypothesis that could not be formulated mathematically as unworthy of serious consideration.

That was clearly not Newton's conviction, certainly not during his most productive years at Cambridge, when, as the unpublished papers reveal, he was absorbed in the search for meaning in ancient esoteric texts. It is clear from his unpublished writings and from accounts of his contemporaries that for Newton, mathematics—like his ingenious physical experiments and carefully crafted scientific instruments—was not primarily a means of discovering truth, but rather a means of demonstrating to lesser minds what he grasped intuitively, albeit often after extended bouts of strenuous introspection. Keynes cites a well-known anecdote involving the astronomer Halley, who inquired of Newton how he knew one of the fundamental laws of planetary motion. He wanted to know specifically if he had proved it. Newton was taken aback by the direct question. It was something he felt he had always known, but he was sure he could find a proof of it in a few days, which he subsequently did.[8]

Today it is known that Newton, a notorious recluse during his productive years at Cambridge, considered himself a member of a secretive brotherhood that sought to decipher the mysteries encrypted in ancient texts. Keynes used the word "addict" to describe the power the esoteric tradition held over the physicist. But as Newton moved into his post-academic life as the almost universally acknowledged "Sage of Europe," his important contributions to science behind him, he took great pains to not undermine the foundation of his fame. The monolithic structure of mathematics and logic he created became the gold standard against which all future scientific theorizing would be measured. In Newton's much-celebrated post-academic life there was no evidence of the passion for esoteric knowledge that occupied him during his productive years at Cambridge. Goethe could not have known that Newton was a kind of anti-Faust who had wrestled his passion for esoteric knowledge to the ground. He saw Newton in essentially the same light as he depicted Wilhelm Meister's foil in the novel, Werner, the wholesale merchant who could find value

---

[8]I recall reading some years ago a somewhat different account of this incident. The greatest scientific minds of seventeenth century Europe were searching for a theory of gravitation, and Newton, the historian noted wryly, had lost it!

only in things that could be itemized on the left side of a balance sheet.

Although Betrand Russell considered Leibniz one of the supreme intellects of all time, [9] the German polymath and Newton's bitter rival was cruelly satirized by Voltaire in his still-eminently-readable *Candide*. Voltaire's masterpiece, one of the most widely read works in the corpus of French literature, stands as an object lesson on the danger to which truth seekers expose themselves when they appear to stray from the currently accepted scientific paradigm. Candide's long-suffering tutor in philosophy, Pangloss, is a caricature of Leibniz, whom Voltaire pilloried for his irrepressible but apparently unfounded optimism in the face of natural disasters, disease and all manner of human avarice, mean-ness and depravity.

It should be pointed out that Voltaire had earlier emerged as the most important popularizer of Newton's ideas on the continent. The full title of his delightful picaresque novel is *Candide, ou l'Optimisme*, which was translated into English in 1759 as *Candide: or, All for the Best*, and again in 1762 as *Candide: or, The Optimist*. The lightning rod for the brutal satire was Leibniz' *Théodicée*, the only full-length monograph the German polymath published in his lifetime. This work, along with his posthumously published *Monadologie*, made Leibniz an easy target for lesser minds who, lulled into complacency by the rapid advance of technology underwritten by the progress of science, were not willing to give serious thought to the difficult questions he con-fronted head-on.

The problem of evil, particularly of the natural kind, was considered by many leading intellectuals of the time to be an argument for atheism. The syllogism goes like this: God and evil

---

[9] *A History of Western Philosophy*, Simon and Schuster, New York, (1945), p.581.

are incompatible, but evil clearly exists; God, therefore, does not exist. Failure to comprehend this logic was offered as evidence of extreme simple-mindedness.

The argument continues to resonate with many thinkers today who often appear more concerned with avoiding the label "naïve" or "sentimental" than with confronting the profound philosophical questions that motivated Leibniz. Voltaire, of course, could not have known, any more than Goethe, that Newton, in his most productive years, was at least as concerned as Leibniz with making sense of the human condition. Like his somewhat older compatriot Milton, Newton privately saw himself as a prophet concerned with "justifying the ways of God to men." But unable to capture esoteric knowledge in his newly fashioned mathematical net, he sealed the evidence of his Miltonesque struggle in a trunk. Leibniz, in contrast, incautiously published the results of his study for all the world to see.

In his autobiographical masterpiece, *Dichtung und Wahrheit* (*Poetry and Truth*), Goethe admitted he did not enjoy reading Leibniz while studying law as a young man at the University of Leipzig; but his mature worldview has enough in common with the philosopher of optimism to make his antipathy toward Newton readily understandable. According to his eighteenth-century followers, Newton's universe was purely mechanical, made of material objects that moved deterministically according to the laws of classical physics. In Newton's universe, mechanical interaction is fundamental, a feature which gives rise to the twin conundrums of action at a distance and the mind-body problem—the apparent ability of a non-material mind to interact with matter. By the late nineteenth century classical physicists, as impressed with the ability of science to underwrite technology as we are today, typically addressed such questions by declaring them non-scientific, uninteresting, meaningless, or simply based on illusion.

Many modern scientists with decidedly secular or atheistic worldviews seem content to follow their classical forebears in this regard. But in his *Monadologie*, Leibniz—co-inventor, with Newton, of the calculus, without which classical physics is unthinkable—had imagined a thoroughly non-Newtonian universe composed entirely of immaterial "monads" whose movement reflects, not interaction, but a pre-established harmony with all other monads in the universe.

If the universe had turned out to be less mysterious, less alive and less enigmatic than quantum theory has discovered it to be, the idea that each monad would somehow *know* the position and movement of all other monads could be dismissed as patently absurd. But already in the nineteenth century experimental evidence and theoretical considerations began to suggest to thoughtful scientists that many phenomena—most particularly, apparently instantaneous action at a distance—could not be understood in terms of material bodies interacting in space. The majestic movement of Foucault's pendulum suspended from the dome of the Panthéon in Paris, for example, confronted thoughtful observers with the mystery of inertia in a visceral way.

What, Newton had wondered, could hold the moon in orbit around the Earth other than the knowledge specified in his equations? Nothing mechanical came to mind, causing him to confess that he would frame no hypothesis. Mach's reinterpretation of Newton's spinning-bucket experiment suggested that inertia itself was the physical embodiment of the knowledge encoded in the law of universal gravitation; for Mach, inertia somehow instantiates a massive body's relationship to the distribution of mass in the rest of the universe.

Although Mach most likely did not allow his speculation to go in this direction, in such a world, any gravitating body would be like one of Leibniz' monads in this sense: its interaction with other massive bodies would be explainable, not mechanically, but in terms of its implicit—and essentially instantaneous—awareness or knowledge of its relationship to those other bodies, the overwhelming preponderance of which includes those vastly distant bodies referred to somewhat poetically as the fixed stars. Massive bodies as monad-like entities embodying knowledge of their relationship to other massive bodies was clearly not an idea that fit comfortably in the worldview of classical physics.

This Leibniz-friendly notion—that material bodies could coordinate their behavior instantaneously without physical interaction—was an idea that Einstein considered so absurd that he made it the basis for his last and most famous challenge to quantum physics. He was not particularly concerned about the action-at-a-distance problem that had troubled Newton: he had dealt with that issue to his own satisfactions in his Special and General Theories of Relativity and felt he could use results obtained there to demonstrate a weakness or incompleteness in quantum theory. In a world described by his two eminently successful theories, there simply could be no instantaneous action at a distance. Effects could propagate maximally at the speed of light in a vacuum.

But whereas Einstein believed to have solved the action-at-a-distance problem, quantum theory had dealt with the other great conundrum left untouched by classical physics—the mind-body problem—in a most troubling way. The big game Einstein was after, therefore, was not the action-at-a-distance implication of quantum theory, but the quantum enigma itself—the essentially mystical idea that physical reality might somehow be observer-dependent. After all, if the measurable properties or qualities of physical matter depended in any way on the subjective experience of being observed, the goal of capturing them in a completely objective mathematical net is placed permanently out of reach. Einstein's physical intuition—as well, perhaps, as the huge emotional investment he had in his own theory of gravity—told him there had to be a flaw in a theory that made such a prediction.

The mathematical formalism in which the new theory was stated predicted a phenomenon—quantum entanglement—that suggested that two entangled micro particles would form a single entity in the sense that acting on one would affect the other *instantaneously*, despite significant (even vast) spatial separation. That prediction was the chink in the empirical armor of the otherwise stupendously successful theory that Einstein proposed to pierce. Einstein's unshakeable conviction that quantum phenomena were objectively real—that they did not depend on measurement or any kind of interaction to realize the qualities they were observed to have—led him to believe that there must be some hidden variables on the micro level not described by quantum theory in its present state. In other words, in his view, if these hidden variables were only known it could be possible to explain the *illusion* that quantum-entangled particles flout the speed limit imposed by his theories of relativity.

Physicists sometimes use the example of a pair of gloves that have been separated, packaged identically and sent to distant locations, to suggest what a hidden-variable theory—more properly thought of as a *local* hidden-variable theory—might look like. If you were to receive one of these identically-wrapped packages you could not determine the handedness of the glove it contained until you performed the actual experiment of opening the package and looking inside. At that point you would also obtain knowledge as to the handedness of the distant glove, instan-taneously, without interacting with it. Observing the handedness of the glove here would not cause the distant glove to assume the proper handedness. Each glove was either right- or left-handed all along—only your knowledge would change upon performing the experiment. Prior to opening your package you would have had to guess as to the handedness of the glove inside—with a 50% chance of guessing correctly.

But a successful hidden-variable theory would do more than solve the instantaneous action-at-a-distance problem, which, as noted, was not a problem for Einstein, but rather a key to unraveling the quantum enigma: If the property that an experiment was set up to determine—the handedness of a quantum particle, for example—really existed in the particle and was merely hidden from view in the current theory, a successful hidden-variable theory would also show a way around the Heisenberg uncertainty relation, which forms the bedrock of quantum theory. Hidden-variable theories therefore became a kind of Holy Grail for theorists seeking to ground physics in real, independently existing *things* that could be described in completely objective terms.

For several years after the Second World War, David Bohm—the physicist quoted approvingly in the Introduction—worked at Princeton's Institute for Advanced study, where he had ample opportunity for an exchange of ideas with Einstein. In 1951 he produced a mathematically coherent hidden-variable theory that reproduced all the predictions of quantum theory without requiring the involvement of a conscious observer to collapse the wave function. In other words, in Bohm's theory, complementary qualities such as handedness that, in the standard interpretation of quantum theory, did not inhere in the particles until they were observed, were objectively real.

Einstein, who would live another two years after Bohm published his theory, was undoubtedly pleased, although Bohm was able to obtain his result only by introducing an assumption that must have made Einstein wince: Bohm purchased the reality of complementary properties (like handedness) in quantum-entangled particles at the price of assuming instantaneous action-at-a-distance.

The idea that physical reality is non-local goes against professional intuition honed over decades of study and intimate familiarity with the amazing extent to which the structure of theoretical physics—based ultimately on the assumption of interaction and casual relationships expressible in differential equations—forms a coherent whole. Professionals conversant with this fantastic corpus of scientific theory cannot escape having their intuition shaped by it.

I am not a physicist, so I cannot draw upon their well-founded physical intuition; but, in consolation, neither is my thinking overly constrained by it. I do share the widespread reluctance of mainstream theoreticians to endorse Bohm's system, but for a radically different reason: In contrast to many physicists, at a gut level I react negatively to the assumption that physical reality is strictly local. If my intuition had not already developed in this direction, the visit of Helen's ghost the night she was murdered a thousand miles to the north would have led me to question this assumption. Bohm's explicit assumption that physical reality is non-local, far from being a mark against his theory, is, for me, an attractive feature. It is, moreover—and this is worth noting—an assumption that thirty years of intensely scrutinized experimentation appears to have substantiated.

In 1964 the Irish physicist John Stewart Bell, intrigued by Bohm's reinterpretation of quantum physics in terms of hidden variables, proved a mathematical inequality that set limits to experimentally observable correlations between microevents in a locally-real "classical" world—that is, in a world, such as the one described by Einstein's General Theory of Relativity—where effects cannot propagate faster than the speed of light. What inspired Bell was the fact that Bohm's hidden-variable theory reproduced all the predictions of wave mechanics while preserving the physical reality of properties of complementary elementary particles. In other words, Bohm's theory showed a theoretical way around logical absurdities such as Schrödinger's alive/dead cat that bothered Einstein so much. If properties of entangled quantum particles are real—like the handedness of each of a matching pair of gloves concealed in separate packages—then Schrödinger's cat would be alive or dead inside the box, whether the experimenter opened the box to check on it or not. It would not exist in a superposed alive-dead state waiting for the consciousness of the experimenter to cause it to collapse into one state or the other.

Bell's proof of his famous inequality opened the door for experimentalists to begin designing real-world analogues of Einstein's thought experiment, which, in effect became tests of Bohm's assumption of non-locality. If the experimental results supported the Bell inequality, then the conclusion Einstein drew from his thought experiment—that quantum theory is incomplete—would be vindicated; the possibility of describing reality in completely objective terms would remain viable. If, on the other hand, experimental results violated the Bell inequality, then the assumption of non-locality underlying Bohm's theory would be justified.

As physicists are fond of pointing out, quantum theory has passed every empirical test to which it has been subjected. Thirty years of experimental results violate the Bell inequality. Diehard proponents of local realism continue to look for weaknesses in the experiments, principally in their mathematical or logical underpinnings, but most physicists appear to be convinced by the experimental evidence that physical reality is non-local.[10] In other

---

[10] Klingman, siding with Einstein and de Broglie on this issue, is not one of these physicists. In an email he referred me to his 2012 FQXi essay, "The Nature of the Wave Function," which is far too technical for me to

words, the consensus among physicists is that, what I do here (for example, observe a photon) can have an instantaneous effect on a distant entangled photon, even on the other side of the observable universe. The explanation is that the entangled particles, despite their spatial separation, form part of a single whole.

****

Let us review some of the ideas we have been discussing as a backdrop for the more philosophical and romantic pictures of reality that Leibniz and Goethe embraced:

1. If, as most physicists believe, quantum entanglement is real, *space* is clearly not what it appears to be.
2. Since matter is mostly empty space (whatever that is), it, too, is clearly not what it appears to be.
3. Since time does not flow for photons—which, from their perspective, may cross the entire visible universe instantly—and because there are enclaves within this visible universe that are surrounded by event horizons where, from our perspective, time grinds to a halt, *time itself* is clearly not what it appears to be.
4. Finally, since virtually all of the mass of elementary particles is not inherent in them, but derives from what they are doing, *mass* is clearly not what it appears to be.

What we see here is the universe forcing scientists to confront the mysterious nature of the reality Newton had hoped to grasp with his decades-long study of alchemy and esoteric literature. I am convinced that Leibniz, if he were alive, would be more comfortable with these scientific findings than Voltaire, or even

_____

evaluate. I like the general thrust, however, which is that the wave function is physically real.

Newton, whereby I do not mean to detract anything from the French writer's brilliant satire of naïve optimism or the incomparable English physicist's enduring legacy. Leibniz, un-cowed by Newton's brilliance, was not naïve, and his optimism was not of the naïve kind. When Leibniz wrote of the best of all possible worlds, that is exactly what he meant. For Leibniz, the best world is "optimal," given certain constraints. But these constraints should not be viewed as limiting God's power; rather, these constraints would reflect His divine intention, the way a sculptor constrains potentiality when creating a work of art, destroying many to create one. Leibniz reasoned that it would surely be possible for God to create a world without evil and pain, but it was not clear to him that a world sanitized of evil would necessarily be better or superior to the one that, in his view, God actually did create.

The enlightened mortals Voltaire appealed to in *Candide* might judge a world without evil and pain superior to the world of their experience. But the question is not how such a world appears to mere mortals, who, as Paul wrote, see through a glass darkly,[11] but how such a world would appear to the God who created it. And, more pointedly, how would such a world appear to us if we were somehow able to assume the divine perspective. Would, indeed, a world free of pain and suffering be capable of producing beings capable of viewing it from such vantage point? Could consciousness emerge and rise to that level in a world where there is no need to consider the consequences of one's actions on others because in such a world untoward consequences—pain, evil or suffering—were not permitted?

This is *my* real question, which I think may have motivated Leibniz in his *Théodicée*: Could a world with no pain and suffering—

---

[11]He continues importantly as follows: "now I know in part; but then shall I know even as also I am known." [1 Corinthians 13:12]

a world without evil—be compatible with the emergence of consciousness that derives ultimately from experiencing the
consequences of one's action? Could such a world be compatible
with free will? Could a world innocent of pain and suffering and
the experience of loss be capable of calling independent conscious
beings into existence capable of participating in genuine love
relationships? It just so happens that *our* world, *this* vale of tears,
the spacetime of our experience, does engender such beings. Yes,
there is evil, pain and suffering in our world, but there is also love
and sacrifice. Where does that come from? It is not at all clear to
me that a world purged of evil and suffering, a Garden of Eden, as
it were, could accomplish what this world accomplishes.

I am reminded of one of the most famous lines from Goethe's
most famous literary masterpiece, his closet drama *Faust*. The
legendary alchemist, despairing of his ability to comprehend the
true nature of reality, decided to turn to a source of esoteric
knowledge for help, to the "secret-heavy book by Nostradamus'
own hand."[12] As Goethe wrote these words he could not have
known that Newton himself had, in his search for understanding
during his most productive time at Cambridge, spent years
analyzing this and other founts of esoteric wisdom. In this scene,
Faust has just succeeded in conjuring the Earth Spirit, whom he
addresses as his equal, both participating, as Faust points out, in
the divine essence.

Mephistopheles quickly puts Faust in his place:

Du gleichst dem Geist, den du begreifst,
Nicht mir!
(You resemble the spirit you comprehend,
Not me!)

---

[12] This "geheimnisvolle Buch/ von Nostradamus' eigner Hand."

To emphasize the important point Mephistopheles is making, Goethe causes Faust, in his moment of triumph—he has, after all, just succeeded in conjuring the Earth Spirit—to be interrupted by his dull assistant, Wagner, for whom he harbors the utmost contempt. Mephistopheles quickly makes it clear to Faust that, compared to him, the alchemist is indistinguishable from his despised famulus.

This is Goethe's one-line answer Voltaire's brilliant but superficial dismantling of Leibniz' optimistic philosophy—a further sharpening of his pointed criticism of Newton quoted above. Goethe knew well what nature, what our living universe, can do. Among other things, this universe brings forth unique, powerful and unfathomably mysterious monads such as Newton, Leibniz and my grandmother Terry; it also stages terrible, emotion-laden drama like the one my son experienced at age 13, when he accidentally crushed his pet parakeet between a door and its jamb. Compared to the Earth Spirit that they would engage in dialogue, a Faust or a Newton or any other scientist is indistinguishable from a hack or factotum.

The diverging posthumous reputations of Newton and Leibniz provide an object lesson in the danger scientists incur in the post-enlightenment secular world when they acknowledge the mysterious nature of our living, spirit-filled universe. Newton, lionized by Voltaire as the consummate realist who described the world in terms of inert physical bodies acted upon by external forces, spent the last quarter century of his life in comfortable circumstances, hailed by the educated world as the "Sage of Europe." Leibniz, whom Voltaire caricatured for his supposedly naïve, essentially mystical view of nature, spent the last years of his life ignored by the intellectual and scientific community to which he had made enduring contributions.

Although he was a lifetime member of the Royal Society and the Berlin Academy of Sciences, neither organization honored his passing. Upon his death, Leibniz was buried in an unmarked grave, apparently in a simple wooden casket. Fifty years would pass before a marker was set, but even today there is no irrefutable evidence that the bones buried below this marker belong to the farsighted German polymath and philosopher of optimism.

www.ingramcontent.com/pod-product-compliance
Lightning Source LLC
La Vergne TN
LVHW051508080426
835509LV00017B/1985